The Lost Anchor

Kent Welch

The Lost Anchor

Contact Information for the Author:
kentrwelch@protonmail.com
https://www.facebook.com/kentrwelch/

ISBN. 978-1-7358139-0-5

First Edition. September 2020

The Lost Anchor

Acknowledgments

A writer will always miss his mark when he writes a book about the greatest book. Even the most gifted writers (among whom I am not) will find himself frustrated with his lack of ability to capture the fullness of what God has revealed in His written word, and through His living Word. Nevertheless, God has through the years compelled men and women to write and encourage one another to stay the course and remain true to the Scriptures.

In writing such books, it is advisable to seek the counsel of trusted friends who will tell you the truth, keep you honest, and help you as the writer to remain on as straight a course as possible. The Bible is not a book to be trifled with, and it is not a book about which one should write absent of a sense of the awesomeness of the task. Acutely aware of my own limitations and weaknesses, alongside the sheer size and responsibility of the task, I enlisted such friends to read this book and offer their insights, thoughts, suggestions, and edits. Without them, this book might never have been published and would have been far less than what it is. With these thoughts in mind, I want to acknowledge the help of brother Todd Larkey, Elder Douglas Skinner, Elder James Keen, and my wife Sarah. You each have my sincere thanks, and I pray you have God's blessing for your assistance with the completion of this work.

To my church family, thank you for your ongoing encouragement and for the love we share in the Lord. I publish this book with the prayer that it will be an honor to our Lord and that it will be a help to our shared witness to the world.

Forward

The Holy Bible has weathered the tests of time for thousands of years. This longevity has not been attained by the efforts of mankind. Although men such as John Wycliffe and William Tyndale have given their lives towards its survival, its ultimate preservation and proliferation is from the hand of its author. Matthew 24:35 *"Heaven and earth shall pass away, but my words shall not pass away."* These words, inspired by the Holy Spirit to be penned by human hands, have an eternal purpose, and have withstood all tests because God has willed it to be so. The Written word's purpose is to reveal to us the Living Word who became flesh and dwelt among us (*Jn 1.14*). The Living Word, Jesus Christ the Messiah, has as His motivation, agape love. It is agape love which led Him to humble Himself to die at the hands of sinful men in order to fulfill His Father's will, pay the sin penalty for the fallen human race and pave mankind's path back to proper communion with God. This Holy word tells us of God's love toward sinners through the wonderful plan of redemption. The word of God is as perfect as the sacrifice which was required for our sin debt. It is as absolute and complete as the plan of salvation and has as its subject and theme, Jesus and Him crucified. The Bible's perfection is further illustrated in its last chapter by a stern warning to those who would attempt to alter it in Revelation 22:18-19.

The Holy Bible is perfectly suited for our consumption. The One who fashioned our first father from the dust of the earth is the author of this holy book. Its words are meant for us. The word tells us who God is and who we are, thus defining the great sin chasm which separates us from God. It speaks of the cure for sin found in

Jesus and the optimal way to live life more abundantly following the new birth which Jesus described to Nicodemus (*John 3*). It describes the love God has for sinners and the awful judgment and punishment which awaits sin and those unwilling to repent of their sin and trust fully the work and person of Christ Jesus. It teaches of things which happened long ago, and shows us the state of the world currently, and tells us what to expect in the future. It is a perfect volume of truth.

God's word is also absolute. Absolute is defined as: *"something that is not dependent upon external conditions for existence or for its specific nature, size, etc."* God's word is as sure as He is, and its truth is based upon His attributes and nature. God will not change or age or vary from century to century (*Jam. 1.17, Heb.13.8*) which makes God's word unique among all the other writings, even without consideration of its authorship.

Absolute truth is real, it is relevant, it is found exclusively in the Holy Bible and is revealed by the Holy Spirit. This, of course, is not popular in today's America. We are told that all things are relative, and truth is being actively sacrificed on the altar of political correctness. Now, more than ever, we must recognize that we are *"…in this world, but not of this world"*. As the distinction between truth and falsehood becomes clearer, we must be found squarely set and anchored in the absolute truth of God's word. Anything less is failure.

The value of this book, *The Lost Anchor*, is found in its subject, and the timeliness of the lessons contained herein. The world is so very obviously changing at a faster pace and in a decidedly more wicked direction than at any time in recent history. These changes have emboldened the wicked and cowed many of God's people. But uneasy and uncomfortable times should never defeat the people of God. If history has shown us anything, it is that God's people have thrived in the face of persecution and darkness by clinging to the absolute nature of God and His Holy word – the anchor of their souls *and* lives. This book is of immense value as we face the current crossroads of modern American Christianity, and the looming clouds of persecution and open wickedness. History has shown that such times have often swept away individuals, families, communities and even entire nations which were not anchored to the Rock of Jesus Christ - not just in salvation, but in true Christ-centered, Christ-focused, and faith-based living. This volume, I believe, will stand the test of time as it is both timely for American Christianity, and timeless in that it teaches the word of God. Men must be careful when placing pen to paper as thoughts and opinions often change with time, not to mention the likelihood of human error or nefarious motivations for the writing. This is not the case with this book, which I have read thoroughly and endorse completely. Further, I recommend it to you and any you love, especially if they are in possession of heart-felt, know so salvation and make a sincere effort to serve the Lord Jesus Christ.

I have known the author of this book for over thirty years and can personally attest to his life-fruit as a child of God and a God-called minister of the gospel. His life has been a model of sincerity and genuineness in working as a professional, raising a family, preaching the gospel, pastoring churches and living a Holy Spirit-led life. Matthew 7:18-19 says, *"Even so every good tree bringeth forth good fruit; but a corrupt tree bringeth forth evil fruit. A good tree cannot bring forth evil fruit, neither can a corrupt tree bring forth good fruit.*" Jesus said here, during the Sermon on the Mount, that we can know someone's true roots, motivations, and character by the fruit their life bears. I can attest to much fruit borne in the Lord's work by this author. His gift for writing has become a great benefit to God's people. Many of God's children understand these truths, but few are sharing them.

One final reason for why this book is worthy of your time, prayer, and consideration. In knowing the author for most of his life (and mine), I can tell you that these thoughts are not his alone. The Lord has used his mind and heart to pen these words to benefit God's people, and I pray we take advantage of the multitude of hours placed into this work. Brother Kent has a strong mind, but a bigger heart and I promise this project will make you a better Christian and help prepare you for whatever is ahead in this wonderful nation of ours. *"Teaching them to observe all things whatsoever I have commanded you: and, lo, I am with you always, even unto the end of the world. Amen." (Matthew 28:20)*

Soli Deo Gloria.

Elder Douglas W. Skinner
Bowling Green, KY - September 2020

Preface

God had something to say, and He wrote it down. If this statement is true, could there be any words more important than those authored by God Himself? Wouldn't they be words worthy of being read, studied, and treasured above all others? Of course, they would be, just as they have been for more than two millennia. Providentially preserved and unchanged since their penning, they are the words which form the basis of Western civilization. They are words which determine the fate of nations, driving physical prosperity and moral credibility, or crippling prospects and dooming generations. And yet, they are also the words which create family, define love, and offer the only hope of peace and contentment to a broken and humiliated heart. They are the words that bring life and bring it more abundantly, for they are the words that bring Christ. They are the words that anchor us.

It is of little wonder then that these words of God would find themselves under enemy assault. From our governments, through our schools, and even in our pews and behind our pulpits, the authenticity and validity of the Bible has been called into question for generations. The result is a society disconnected from its anchor. We are now adrift, ruled by the ever-changing winds of man's philosophy and political correctness. Biblically minded pastors and counselors have been traded for earthly minded therapists. Heartfelt repentance for sin has been traded for pills designed to dull senses and quiet anxieties. The Creator's explanation of His creation has been traded for the fickle suppositions of the secular scientist, ironically and cleverly packaged as unassailable truths. In other words, God's never-changing word has been exchanged for the always-changing words of man. And so, we find ourselves with nothing to hold us steady in an unsteady world. No rock upon which to cling in the often-violent storms of life. We are flailing our arms, searching in desperation for something solid to help us remember and define who we are, what we believe, and why we exist. But having rejected the Bible, there is nothing for us to grab onto which will endure beyond the latest whim of man's devising, and we are swept further and further into the churning sea of Relativism.

As troubling as it is to see the greater part of our society leave behind the anchor of Scripture, more troubling still is the sight of Christians doing the same. In misguided attempts to relate to the unbeliever, many within the larger Christian community have distanced themselves from the historical convictions that believers in Jesus Christ have held through the centuries -- convictions on the Bible's divine authorship, in its position as the single source of truth, in its absence of error, its necessity, its clarity, and its sufficiency. Many pastors are now willing to speak in the open about their rejection of these historical tenants of the Christian faith. For every pastor willing to do so, there are likely many others who agree but would never admit to it openly. In the pews of our churches, there are well dressed boys and girls who reject outright the first two chapters of Genesis. They do so in large part because for every minute of the Bible they hear, they hear hours upon hours of secular skepticism. This skepticism comes to them in the classroom, on television, and the digital devices that have overtaken their minds and left them with little ability to think for themselves. In this stew of relativism in which our youth are now swimming, absolute truth is tossed out, leaving nothing but the dry and bitter taste of the empty and cynical opinions of men. If this trend is not reversed soon, our nation will find itself as Israel once did, with a generation who not only did not obey the voice of God, but one who no longer even recognized it.

I have written this book for three primary reasons. First, to obey God. An acute sense of a lack of qualification has attended the writing of this book. But the lack of qualification (real or imagined) is not the central issue. Many have shied away from obedience due to a sense of inadequacy or lack of qualification. Yet, God equips the called more often than He calls the equipped, and I cling to this hope in the completion of this work. Second, I desire to offer encouragement to those who believe the Bible to be what it claims to be but have not had the necessary teaching to confront and counter the accusations of those who attempt to belittle and dismiss it. There is no cause for concern at a close look at Scripture. There are no hidden rocks that once overturned will strike a killing blow to our faith. We will find instead a storehouse of affirmation that our Bibles do in fact contain the very words of God. Third, I pray that God might put this book in the hands of the skeptic. It is my desire to provide reasons for the hope that lies within me and my fellow believers. Many immediately discredit anyone claiming to believe the Bible, thinking them to be simple, naive, or weak-minded. In the pages of this book, I aim to provide evidence that the Christian belief with reference to the Bible is not based on a whim, superstition, or some silly flight of fancy. Rather, it is based on historical evidence, reason, and a faith established in the substantive and real presence of God in the heart. As has been said, faith is not a leap in the dark, it is a leap out of the darkness and into the light. I hope the pages of this book are a source of light in the darkness amid a country that is teetering on the edge of fully losing its way. A nation in great danger of losing its ever-weakening grip on the anchor of truth, the word of God.

Kent Welch

September 2020

The Lost Anchor

CONTENTS

Part One

The Lost Anchor

Chapter 1 - The Removal of the Absolute

"Thy word is true from the beginning. And every one of thy righteous judgments endureth for ever." (Psalm 119:160)

The Absence of the Absolute

If you crave acceptance in America today, there are a few things you must avoid. Chief among these pitfalls, you must never claim truth as absolute, universal, and applicable to every human being. Holding to an absolute truth will see you labeled arrogant, unkind, backward, or worse. While it is acceptable to hold many truths, holding a single, absolute, and universal truth is deemed subversive. You are allowed to find *your* truth, but you must not claim to know *the* truth.

Even the language of truth has changed. Gone are the days in which truth was spoken of as an objective reality. Instead, today we speak in subjective terms. Opinions, feelings, and preferences are more sacred now than objective truth. Phrases like, I feel, I want, and I prefer, are used more often than the phrases I know, I see, and I understand. Perhaps it is time to re-examine what we mean when we speak of truth.

TRUTH[1], *noun*

Conformity to fact or reality*; exact accordance with that which is, or has been, or shall be. The truth of history constitutes its whole value. We rely on the truth of the scriptural prophecies.*

My mouth shall speak truth Proverbs 8.7.

Sanctify them through thy truth; thy word is truth John 17.17.

Though the references to scripture have been notably removed, current dictionaries continue to define the word truth as conformity to fact or reality. This simple definition reminds us that truth defines what is real, but if there is no longer objective truth, but only a relative one, subject to individual interpretations, then is not reality now also subjective? That would appear to be the

---

[1] "truth." webstersdictionary1828.com. Websters Dictionary 1828. Retrieved June 17, 2019.
http://webstersdictionary1828.com/Dictionary/truth

logical conclusion. How, then, can we know what is real when real is subjective? Helpfully, experts in the field now make this unnecessary, telling us we can make things real in our lives simply by willing them into existence. If something is thought to be true, then it is true. I do not dispute the power of the mind to affect how we experience reality. However, it is a distant leap from there to a place where our minds determine reality, opinions become fact, and where subjective imagination becomes objective truth.

This shift is more than a philosophical battleground of the mind or an argument of nomenclature. It involves more than academics mulling weighty topics in their modern Mars' Hill equivalents, coffee houses, lecture halls, and conference rooms. It plays out on playgrounds, in classrooms, and in our homes right under our noses. From video games to movies and television, the line between what is real and what is not has been blurring in our country for generations. Many young people live large portions of their days in a false world that exists only in their minds. Manipulated by the developers of one video game after another, they lose their hold on what is real and what is imaginary. Hollywood portrays a make-believe world where illicit sex has no consequences, drugs do not destroy, and murderers are just misunderstood victims. In today's movies, the good guys are often the bad guys and the bad guys are often the good guys. Up is down. Down is up. Right is wrong. Wrong is right. All of this serves to reinforce the notion that reality is not actually real. Reality is instead what you want it to be. Truth, reality, and fact are now subject to the imagination of man rather than determined by the observable world in which we live.

Of course, reality has a way of forcing itself upon us despite how desperately we might want to wish it away. I can wish that the human body did not break down and weaken with age, but reality is not subject to my wishing. I experience the aches and pains of getting older no matter how much I would prefer to feel young again. What I think and hope for does not change what actually is.

There are times in life when reality does not immediately confront us, and we can ignore it for a time. Sometimes we can ignore it for many years, but reality always plays the final card in this game of denial, and her card always comes up trumps. In 2008, many economies of the West found themselves at the brink of collapse. The remedy? Struggling governments printed more money. Rather than face the pain that would have encouraged a lasting economic correction, they ignored the universal law that spending more than you have is unsustainable. History is littered with nations that have printed their money into worthlessness. Many claim that we are past the financial crisis of 2008. I believe reality just has not caught up with us yet. One thing is certain though; reality will eventually catch up. When it does, we will discover that the only success of 2008 was the successful denial of the fundamental laws of economics. It might be our children and grandchildren who feel the brunt of the blow when reality forces our hand and plays her final card, but reality will have the final call. She always does.

Our Present Position

Having discarded the anchor, we have drifted a long way from where we started. Some see this as a victory. Many in American academia are actively rewriting and redefining our history through a lens absent of the absolute. The belief in the Bible many of our founders held is now considered a fundamental flaw in our society. It was once a helpful reinforcement of our principles to quote their reliance on the Bible, but today, those same quotes are met by accusation, not celebration.

Many of the advances we believe we have made by making truth relative have instead hindered our ability to make real and lasting progress. Our founders established what would become the most prosperous, industrious, and technologically advanced nation in human history. They did this while holding firmly to their belief in the Bible. The United States became the economic, military, and academic gold standard of the world. Millions of people left their homes to come to this land of freedom and opportunity. Most of those who came here found lives of peace and prosperity they never could have otherwise enjoyed. The advances in medicine in the United States have been nothing short of stunning. From developing life-saving vaccines to correcting vision with a laser, our understanding of the human body and how to mend it has reached heights reserved for the science fiction novel in previous generations. The technological, economic, and societal advances made in the United States are without peer anywhere in the world, and at any point in history. And our belief in the Bible has not hindered our progress, it has always been a great enabler of that progress by firmly anchoring us to truth and reality.

I realize it is not politically correct to speak of these things today. We are discouraged from labeling the United States as exceptional. Many believe this statement implies the United States is exceptional because of the people themselves rather than the ideas they espouse, leading to the misconception that other nations are inferior based on who they are rather than on the degree to which their nation conforms to truth. Speaking of American advancements is offensive because the merit for those advances is often misplaced. America is not great because Americans live here. It is great because of the anchor of truth to which our nation has historically held. That anchor is the Bible, which kept us rooted to the absolute. The Bible reminds us there is right and wrong and that a promise made in business is a matter of personal responsibility to God. It is where we learn that God's intention is for a man to commit himself to one woman and love her as Christ loves the church. In Scripture we find the ingredients for a solid home and family. Safely grounded in a family and tethered firmly to the Bible, we became free to explore, discover, and invent like no other people before us.

Our nation no longer holds to the anchor of God's word today and the great progress of yesterday is fading into the past. Satan told us that ridding ourselves of the weight of the Bible would lead to freedom, but all we found was bondage. Many of the technological advances of our age, including the cell phone and social media, have made us slaves to our own thoughts and narcissistic tendencies. We believed that breaking away from Scripture would allow us to find our own way to all that we desired. Instead, we find ourselves lost like never before. An investigation of history shows that where the Bible has been held as the standard, nations have prospered. Where it has been denied, such prosperity has proved an elusive goal. The presence or absence of progress and the advancement of human society has nothing to do with the color of one's skin or the place on the planet where one lives, but it has everything to do with society's disposition toward reality and truth as defined in God's word.

A Steady Progression

This shift in our nation occurred slowly but steadily over many years. We did not go to sleep one night with a solid hold on the absolute truth of the Bible and wake up the next morning without it. It has been slipping away from our grasp slowly over the years. So slowly, in fact, that in the hectic pace of our everyday lives, most did not realize it was happening. Consumed with the trees of everyday life, we did not notice the new and dangerous forest we were entering. Missing the signs, we continued to travel the road to relativism. One road sign after another warned us of problems ahead, but we either missed them, or we ignored them. In the name of progress for progress' sake, we stopped looking at what we were progressing toward. Our

8

government disconnected our currency from the gold standard during the Johnson and Nixon administrations and drove past the signs cautioning us that this road eventually leads to economic ruin. In the 1950's, we began the systematic removal of God, prayer, and the Bible from our public schools and yet we continued sending our children. We ignored the flashing red signals when divorce became an exit strategy for the bored and discontented. We saw corruption gain control over our political systems, but we continued sending the same corrupt politicians back into office with our votes. Many celebrated when the Supreme Court first called the murder of a child a woman's choice in January 1973. One would hope that the number of human beings whose lives have been taken before they ever drew a single breath in this world would be enough to prompt us to pull over and consider where our path has led us. But instead, we seem to only be increasing our speed.

Taking all this in at once should take our spiritual breath away. We can't help but wonder how we got here. Where did we go wrong? When did our course change so dramatically? What political party is to blame? Where has the church been? What have our pastors and preachers been doing while the moral decay continued to spread across the nation? The answers to these questions all tie to the steady disconnection of our society from the anchor of truth found in Scripture. The slowness of the process obscured it from view. With no anchor to hold us, we ended up drifting in the doldrums called the opinions of men. We were so caught up in the business of everyday life we did not notice when the land, the solid ground of truth, disappeared from our view.

The Lost Anchor

We traveled the road that got us here one step, one poor choice, and one compromise at a time. The journey did not go unseen by everyone. Many saw the dangerous path we were taking and encouraged us to change direction. These men and women reminded us that though we had drifted a long way from where we started, we could look to the heavens and reset our earthly bearings once again. But the voices of warning were marginalized and the voices that supported the removal of God's word from our nation have largely prevailed.

Assessing our nation's current situation illuminates a frightening landscape. We have made one wrong decision after another without the guiding light of the Bible. We grope around in the dark trying unsuccessfully to find our way. Our political system appears to be on the brink of ruin and many politicians act more like petulant children than leaders worthy of our respect and confidence. Our schools fill the minds of our young people with the idea that they are nothing more than highly evolved animals, and they owe their lives to unfeeling, unthinking, and even accidental processes. It is no wonder that so many live their lives with no real meaning, hope, or purpose. What meaning, hope, or purpose can there be if we are all here by accident? Men act like women, and women act like men. The gender identity crisis in America is not new. Though it is no longer obscured from our view as it once was, it is merely the natural progression of what has been taking shape behind the scenes for decades. When masculinity became wrong for a man but right for a woman, and femininity became wrong for a woman but right for a man, the gender identity crisis was already running at full steam.

The family has been devastated by the exchange of the solid ground of Scripture for the shifting sands of humanism. Many children see their fathers and mothers break apart their families for their own selfish purposes. It is no wonder that so many children grow up with the haunting thought their parents loved themselves more than they loved them. The family has been the target of the enemy from the beginning and it will continue to be a target for the rest of time. Broken homes break apart every other facet of life for those impacted, and though this does not mean that a measure of healing and restoration cannot be found after divorce, once a home has been broken the cracks will remain even if the pieces come back together. God purposely allotted a significant portion of the Bible to teach us how to live as families. He taught women how to be wives and mothers and men how to be husbands and fathers. He taught children to honor their parents and He taught us all to love one another sacrificially by putting our needs aside to see to the needs of others. We set aside the recipe for a happy and solid home when we set aside the Bible. The family unit was the first institution God ordained and it serves as the central building block upon which all other institutions rely. Structures crumble when the building blocks crack, and the devastation we have seen in our government, schools, corporations, and churches was easily predictable when the family itself began to fall apart.

It is difficult to think of a single institution that has not been dramatically and negatively impacted by the removal of the Bible. We are seeking something solid to keep us steady in the storms of change that blow around us even if most might not see it or admit it. A ships anchor is deployed while in port to secure it safely in place, but even at sea, a ship will deploy its anchor during a storm to steady it amid the waves that would otherwise overturn it. In a similar way, the Bible has kept our nation tied safely to the truth and afloat during the storms of change that have threatened to overwhelm us during our two and a half century voyage. The United States is once again sailing through some turbulent seas, and the waves of relativism are reaching ever new heights. Without the Bible, we are like an anchorless ship in a storm. Every day we take on more water as the waves crash over the bow, stern, port, and starboard sides of the boat. Those who hold to the Bible do the best they can to bail the water, but they often feel like they are fighting a losing battle. We know that ultimately this is not the case. We know God has told us to be, "... *stedfast, unmoveable, always abounding in the work of the Lord, **forasmuch as ye know that your labour is not in vain in the Lord**.*" *(1 Cor. 15.58).* We hold to the promise of God when He tells us to, "*...prove me now herewith, saith the Lord of hosts, If I will not open you the windows of heaven, And pour you out a blessing, that there shall not be room enough to receive it.*" *(Mal 3.10).* And yet, we see the state we are in as a nation and cannot help but wonder how soon we might sink beneath the waves of history. The anchor of the absolute has been removed from our national mindset and this has placed our nation in great peril.

But there is hope. There is hope for every church and every

12

believer who purposes in their heart to cling to God's word. We can choose to stand with Joshua who said,

"...choose you this day whom ye will serve; whether the gods which your fathers served that were on the other side of the flood, or the gods of the Amorites, in whose land ye dwell. but as for me and my house, we will serve the Lord." (Jos. 24.15).

We can say with David, *"I will delight myself in thy statutes: I will not forget thy word."* (*Ps. 119.16*). We can acknowledge that our nation has let go of the Bible and pray for the necessary strength to hold on to it for ourselves, our families, and our churches. This book has been written to encourage us all to do just that.

Chapter 2 - The Impact on Christianity

"Wherewithal shall a young man cleanse his way? By taking heed thereto according to thy word. With my whole heart have I sought thee. O let me not wander from thy commandments. Thy word have I hid in mine heart, That I might not sin against thee." (Psalm 119:9–11)

Christianity Not Immune

Many Christians agree that the definition of truth has undergone a significant change. However, what many Christian people might not acknowledge, or perhaps even see, is that these changes have begun to cripple Christianity itself. The erosion of truth from our society is a significant cause for concern, but more concerning is the devastating impact these changes have had on Christian churches across the nation. Christianity cannot coexist with moral relativism. Any message that denies the absolute nature of truth is not a Christian message, even if the one proclaiming it professes to be Christian. An examination of a cross section of American Christianity reveals that the disease of relativism, previously quarantined outside the walls of Christianity, has now infected many on the inside. Neither pew nor pulpit has proven immune to this malady.

The most prevalent symptom of this sickness is the idea that truth is unknowable. This repackaging of truth has been swallowed whole by many within Christian circles, and alarmingly, and perhaps unknowingly, applied to both God and His redemptive plan. Having accepted a repackaged idea of truth, salvation becomes something about which a person cannot be certain or know for themselves is true or real. Seekers repeat a few verses of Scripture, or a scripted prayer, or perhaps they attend a membership class with every intention of becoming a Christian. Told that their religious exercises have saved them, they reconcile the fact that nothing changed inwardly with the redefined concept of truth as relative and ultimately unknowable. Salvation itself is thus redefined, aided by this altered view of truth. This situation should send a cold chill down the spine of anyone who understands that nothing less than eternity is at stake. The Scriptures tell us plainly that the knowledge of God (salvation) is something we not only *can* know is real, it is something we *must* know is real. "*I think so,*" and "*I hope so,*" simply will not do. Not a single verse of Scripture supports the idea that salvation is something that is unknown. No believer in Scripture left a testimony that they *hoped* they were going to heaven but were not certain. They said they *knew* they would soon see their Lord, and so too must we. (*Jb 19.25, Jn 17.3, Ro 8.16*)

This does not mean moments of doubt do not occur for the true believer. Scripture encourages us to,

> *"Examine [ourselves], whether ye be in the faith; prove your own selves. Know ye not your own selves, how that Jesus Christ is in you, except ye be reprobates?"* (*2 Cor 13.5*)

Doubt of salvation can be a real issue for a child of God, but this only serves to prove the point here being made. If uncertainty of salvation was the expected norm, then there would be no certain and objective truth about which to be uncertain. If Salvation is not ultimately knowable, the doubt of salvation would be nonsensical. I believe each of us intuitively knows that something as grand and essential as salvation is not something which lives in the realm of uncertainty or unknowability. We would call a man who retired without knowing whether his money will last a fool, but how much more foolish and costly is it to leave this world without knowing where you will be the moment after you close your eyes for the final time?

∞

The Bible and Knowing

Abraham was obeying a God he *knew* when he left his home, his family, and everything familiar to him. He was not following a god he did not know or a god of his own imagination. God spoke to Abraham and told him to *"... get thee out of thy country, and from thy kindred, and from thy father's house, unto a land that I will shew thee." (Gen 12.1)* Abraham would not have set out on his journey were it not for this initial experience with God. Some argue that this type of direct interaction between God and man is unique to the Old Testament, but I argue this is not the case. The personal knowledge of God through Christ is a central theme of the New Testament from the opening pages of Matthew to the closing pages of Revelation. Many passages support this assertion, but Jesus' words in Matthew chapter 16 are particularly helpful.

> *"When Jesus came into the coasts of Caesarea Philippi, he asked his disciples, saying, Whom do men say that I the Son of man am? And they said, Some say that thou art John the Baptist. some, Elias; and others, Jeremias, or one of the prophets. He saith unto them, But whom say ye that I am? And Simon Peter answered and said, Thou art the Christ, the Son of the living God. And Jesus answered and said unto him, Blessed art thou, Simon Bar-jona. for flesh and blood hath not revealed it unto thee, but my Father which is in heaven. And I say also unto thee, That thou art Peter, and upon this rock I will build my church; and the gates of hell shall not prevail against it." (Mat. 16.13–18)*

The Lost Anchor

The Gospel is not merely about being a good or religious person; the Gospel is about knowing Jesus. Peter's answer is informative for us all because He did not equivocate or hedge. He was not guessing, hoping, or speculating. The Apostle Paul makes this clear as well, when, writing to Timothy about the persecutions he suffered for Christ, said,

> "...nevertheless I am not ashamed. **for I know whom I have believed** and am persuaded that he is able to keep that which I have committed unto him against that day." (*2 Tim. 1.12*)

These are not Apostles and disciples following Christ blindly. They *knew* Him. They may not have understood everything He said or did, but they knew that He was the Christ, the Son of the living God.

Peter did not answer Jesus' question in Matthew 16:13 by merely stating facts about Him. Peter could have said, "*You are the one who turned water into wine and fed tens of thousands with only five loaves and two fish. You are the one who calmed the storm and walked on water. You are the one who raised the dead and taught us with power and authority like no other.*" Peter could have said all these things, and while they would have been true things to say, they would not have been the right answer to Jesus' question. Jesus' question was not "*What have I done?*" His question was "*Who am I?*" The Gospel is not about merely knowing things Jesus did, or knowing that there is a God, or even acknowledging that Jesus is His Son. The Gospel is about knowing God personally. It is about having a relationship with the living Savior of the world, Jesus Christ.

We should carefully note that Matthew 16 does not present a one-sided knowledge. After Peter answers the Lord's question showing he knew Jesus, Jesus replied and stated His own knowledge of Peter. In verse 18, Jesus says, "*And I say also unto thee, That thou art Peter...*"*(Mat 16.18)* It is as though Jesus is saying, "*Peter, you know me, and I know you, and this two-way, real, and personal relationship is the rock upon which I will build my church.*" The rock Jesus referred to could not have been Peter, a man who would deny Christ three times and who would continue to wrestle with sin. The rock is also not just Christ alone. The entire exchange is about Peter's knowledge of Jesus and Jesus' knowledge of Peter. They knew one another, and the relationship was real. At its heart, this passage is about knowing Jesus.

Reading Matthew 7:21-23 alongside Matthew 16:13-18 shows even more clearly the necessity of a personal knowledge of Christ."

"*Not everyone that saith unto me, Lord, Lord, shall enter into the kingdom of heaven; but he that doeth the will of my Father which is in heaven. Many will say to me in that day, Lord, Lord, have we not prophesied in thy name? and in thy name have cast out devils? and in thy name done many wonderful works? And then will I profess unto them, I never knew you. depart from me, ye that work iniquity.*" (*Mat 7.21– 23*)

Those who will hear Jesus say "*depart from me*" on the day of judgment will be those He never knew. Their religious commitment, their emphatic profession of faith, and all their good deeds will not substitute for the personal knowledge of Christ which is necessary for salvation. Identifying as a Christian is not, by default, the same thing as being a child of God. Matthew 7:22 reveals the thinking of those who will be eternally cast aside: their focus rests on what *they have done* rather than acknowledging what *Christ did* through His sinless life, sacrificial death, and victorious resurrection. Their defense rests on their own works, but the only adequate defense on that great day will be the work Christ alone has done. If you were to speak with someone in heaven today and ask them why they are there, they would immediately point to the Light of the city, Jesus Christ the Lord. Nothing of what they did while here on earth would be mentioned as a reason for their presence in paradise. The words that would follow their pointing finger would be, "*I know Him, and He knows me.*"

Edgar Young Mullins, the fourth president of the Southern Baptist Theological Seminary, wrote about the difference between salvation and a mere intellectual agreement with the Bible in his book, *The Christian Religion in Its Doctrinal Expression*. There he writes,

> "*The Bible is indeed our supreme and authoritative literary source of the revelation of God which leads to salvation. But salvation is not conditioned upon our belief in, or acceptance of, a book. The knowledge of God of which we now speak is not derived from merely reading the pages of the Bible, or*

from the most rigidly scientific interpretation of its teachings. God's revelation of himself to us comes through his direct action upon our spirits. He comes to us in redeeming grace. There is a spiritual transaction within us. We are regenerated by his power, and lifted to a new moral and spiritual level.[2]"

I grew up in the Southern Baptist church. I have many friends and family members who attend Southern Baptist churches, some of whom serve as dedicated pastors who care deeply for their people and for the word of God. I have been blessed many times over in my adulthood by the purposeful teaching in the Bible I received as a child. To this day, I remember with great fondness the godly man who pastored our church in the small town in Missouri where I grew up. His genuineness, careful study, and passion for the Lord was an inspiration to me then and continues to be so today. I fear, though, that for many within the Southern Baptist church and other mainline evangelical churches, the spiritual transaction which occurs within a person at salvation has been forgotten. Yet, books written by E.Y. Mullins, A.W. Tozer, B.H. Carroll, and many other leading Christian voices of the 19th and early 20th Century declared the Biblical view that a spiritual experience with God is essential for salvation. The strong resurgence of Calvinism (*predestination*) in our day is due in large

_____

[2]Mullins, E. Y. (1917). The Christian Religion in Its Doctrinal Expression (p. 41). Philadelphia; Boston; St. Louis; Los Angeles; Chicago; New York; Toronto: Roger Williams Press

part to the rejection of the extreme Arminianism (*free will*) that took shape in America during the greater part of the 20th Century. The emptiness of the idea that man can simply make a decision to accept Christ apart from a real and experiential transaction taking place in the heart is showing up in the spiritual shallowness that resides in so many churches across America. The theological pendulum is swinging back hard toward Calvinism, and if history is any judge, it will over-correct by removing the necessity of the volition of man in salvation. Yet, the point remains that many today are seeing through the hollow promises that man, by his decision alone, can be saved.

Many pages could be added to this book referencing verse after verse that teach salvation as something which is known, experienced, and certain in the heart. Two particularly powerful passages are 1 Peter 2:9 and John 5:24.

> *"But ye are a chosen generation, a royal priesthood, an holy nation, a peculiar people; that ye should shew forth the praises of him who hath called you out of darkness into his marvellous light." (1 Pet 2.9)*

If salvation is a calling out of darkness into marvelous light, then surely, we must know when this has occurred in our lives. Surely this speaks to an observable experience of the inward man. How could we truly encounter the Light of the world and find that within us there remains only darkness?

> *"Verily, verily, I say unto you, He that heareth my word, and believeth on him that sent me, hath everlasting life, and shall*

not come into condemnation; but is passed from death unto life." (Jn 5.24)

If salvation is a passing from death to life, how is it possible to be unaware of this rebirth? Surely going from spiritual death to spiritual life involves a spiritual change that is experienced and recognized. This verse infers a time and place in which we went from death to life. It does not speak of a process of time or a slow restoration of health. Jesus said that those who hear His word and believe in Him pass from death to life. He does not say that the believer merely begins a journey back to health. We pass from death to life at salvation. We do not just begin to get better; God makes us altogether new by the regenerating work of the Spirit of God. When we recover from physical sickness, we feel a difference in our body, and we know that we are better. We do not just think or hope our health has improved. We know that it has and the way we feel bears witness to the truth of the matter. How much more different then should we feel when we go from being dead spiritually to being alive in Christ? How much more obvious must such a reality be within us when we have not merely gone from being sick to having health restored, but have gone from being dead to being alive?

If these thoughts are new to you, I encourage you to think and pray. If they are new to you, know that they are not new thoughts from Scripture. Do you know Christ? Have you seen His light? Or is there still only darkness within you spiritually? Are you alive in Christ or are you dead in your sin? Do you know Jesus, or do you only know facts about Him? Did God do a work in your heart, or did you just perform a religious work of man to secure your salvation? These are the most important questions you will ever answer.

∞

Christianity Without an Absolute

A large part of the Christian world today speaks of salvation with much less clarity and conviction than does the Scripture. Many present an ambiguous message of salvation rather than the clear message presented in the Bible. The differences are striking, so sharp, in fact, that it is difficult to understand how this situation came to be. The answer is due in part to the subtle, but deadly change to the definition of truth itself. Some will say, "*Your salvation included a great experience with God but that's not how it happened for me.*" Can we not hear in this the influence of the altered definition of truth? Isn't this statement strikingly to, "*That's true for you, but it's not true for me*"? The experience of salvation will be unique for each of us. Some will find God in a church service; others at home or driving to work. Some will show a lot of outward emotion while others will show little. Some will already understand much about the Bible, but others may know almost nothing. However, according to the Bible, all who are born again have a personal knowledge of Christ and have experienced the new birth which He said was essential for anyone to be saved.

Many pastors and teachers today say that we must not base

our assurance of salvation on our subjective experience. I agree with them, but only to a point. We should not base our assurance of salvation on our *subjective* experiences. My feelings, my heart, my emotions, and my mind can all mislead me if I do not exercise care and discernment regarding those experiences. Jeremiah tells us that, *"The heart is deceitful above all things, and desperately wicked. Who can know it?" (Jer. 17.9)* There are many who have had a subjective, *emotional* experience that they consider salvation. Many effective speakers have used precisely planned music and stories that tug at the heart to manipulate the emotions of their hearers, making way for human emotion to be mistaken for the Spirit's work and salvation to be declared when true salvation never came. At the other end of the spectrum lies the subjective *intellectual* experience. This occurs when a person agrees with the moral and ethical tenets of Christianity, but there is no true inward knowledge of Christ. True Christianity is more than just an ethical or moral code - much, much more. One can agree that the Ten Commandments are the best way to govern a society and yet not know the One who first etched those commandments in tablets of stone. Having been uniquely crafted by God, each of us is a unique blend of emotion and intellect, but many of us lean more prominently toward one or the other. Those leaning toward passion can make their intellectually leaning neighbors uncomfortable, while those same intellectuals can prove to frustrate the passionate, but one needs the other. What practical use would right knowledge be without the passion necessary to live according to that knowledge? What damage would passion do without the guidance and governance of right knowledge? God has given us passion and reason. Our reason should govern our passion, but our reason should never become a lifeless code of conduct obeyed robotically with no fire in our hearts. Whichever direction we lean, we need to take care that we do not base our assurance of salvation on a *subjective* experience. Because something *felt right emotionally*, or *seemed right intellectually*, does not by itself mean we were born again.

Yet all of this does not mean that an experience is unnecessary. My response to those who warn against the use of subjective experience as an assurance of salvation is that not all experiences are subjective. Many experiences begin with objective truth and end with objective realities that affect us for the rest of our lives. Yet they remain true *experiences*. Salvation is an objective experience that affects us for the rest of our lives and determines our eternity. The objective component of the experience of salvation is a *personal relationship* with God that did not exist prior to the experience. Where there was no inward connection with God before salvation, there is a real and observable relationship with Him after salvation. The relationship is the objective reality that we must base our assurance of salvation upon, and a relationship is an inherently experiential activity. The question then goes back to our earlier discussion from Matthew 16, "*Do you know Jesus, and does He know you?*" If you do, when did you meet?

How have we arrived at this place of confusion on this fundamental doctrine of the Bible? How has that which is so plain in Scripture become so obscure in so many pulpits and pews of

American Christianity? The changed definition of truth, one which scorns the absolute, provides the rationale for this destructive ambiguity. The Scriptures are clear and definite on the teaching of salvation. They do not present a salvation that is relative to a person, time, or place. God is unchanging and so too is His plan of salvation. God does not change salvation to accommodate for the times or our changing attitudes. Jesus told Nicodemus, "...*unless one is born again, he cannot see the kingdom of God*" (*Jn 3.3*) This can only mean what it says. There is no difficulty in the translation, or nuance in the Greek that could allow for a variety of different interpretations. To reach Heaven, one must be born again.

We often think Satan works to deny the truth openly, and certainly he does, but he often takes an even more crafty and deadly approach. He has worked with patience over many decades to remove from our understanding the absolute nature of truth. Rather than confront and deny the truth, he redefines it. When truth becomes relative or subjective, that redefinition deals a heavy blow to the cause of Christianity. It is time to reconnect to our anchor, the word of God, to reclaim a connection with the absolute and confront the lie of relativism.

Chapter 3 - The Bible and the Absolute

"Thy righteousness is an everlasting righteousness, And thy law is the truth." (Psalm 119:142)

A Changing Perspective

There was a time in America when even unbelievers looked at the Bible with a measure of respect. Many held the preacher in esteem as a man charged by God to speak His words, and the preacher earned that respect through his awareness that his task was a *calling* to proclaim God's word and not merely a *profession*. It was once a solemn act to place your hand on the Bible and promise to tell the truth in a court of law. There was a reverence and deference given to the Bible. However, our nation has drifted away from God and the respect for the Bible and those who believe it is largely a part of our past. The preacher is no longer seen as a serious-minded man of God who speaks the truth of God. His voice is one that many believe should be silent in favor of the self-proclaimed experts in science, philosophy, and psychology. In church pews across the country, more and more professing Christians believe the pastor incapable of speaking to the issues of our day with Scripture. Pastors, sensing this shift in the pew, often call upon authorities outside the Bible to lend credibility to their sermons. It is as though they have forgotten that their mandate is to preach the word of God, nothing more and nothing less. Their sermons often reinforce in the minds of their hearers that the word of God is insufficient on its own. It is one thing to use sources outside the Bible to *illustrate* the Bible's message. It is another to use them to *prove* the Bible's message. In the first case, the Bible stands on its own. In the second, it only stands with help. There is a subtle but deadly difference between the two.

These modified views of the Bible have resulted in its near complete removal from public discourses in our society. Our politician's distance themselves from the Bible for fear of losing votes. In the name of tolerance, corporate America does not tolerate the Bible. Public schools no longer have room for the Bible in their curriculum. The absence of the Bible from our government, the workplace, and the classroom has created enormous pressure on the church and the individual believer to change their view of the Bible. However, as we will see later in this book, to view the Bible as less than absolute truth is to modify the essential claim the Bible makes for itself.

∞

It is troubling to watch this happen in our country, but we should recognize that this is not the first time the attempt to reshape and remove the word of God has occurred. The first tactic Satan used to tempt man was to change what God had said. Satan began his deception of Eve with a question designed to confuse and cast doubt on what God had clearly told her. Satan came to Eve and asked, "...*hath God said, Ye shall not eat of every tree of the garden?*" *(Gen. 3.1)*. Eve responded that God had told them,

"*We may eat of the fruit of the trees of the garden. But of the fruit of the tree which is in the midst of the garden, God hath said, Ye shall not eat of it, neither shall ye touch it, lest ye die.*" *(Gen. 3.2-3)*.

After casting *doubt* with his first question, Satan then moves to *deny* God's word. He told Eve,

"*Ye shall not surely die. For God doth know that in the day ye eat thereof, then your eyes shall be opened, and ye shall be as gods, knowing good and evil.*" *(Gen. 3.4-5)*.

This approach proved successful for Satan, and he talked a sinless man and woman out of paradise with an assault on the word of God. Doubt and denial of God's word represent core weapons in Satan's arsenal, and he continues to use them to great effect today. The doubt of God's word in our nation has turned to outright denial, and this denial has left a large part of our society in a smoldering ruin. Ruin and destruction are always the result of the denial of God's word. This was true for Adam and Eve in the beginning, and it remains true for us today.

∞

The Bible's Claim to Absolute Truth

The denial of the existence of absolute truth has led to the rejection of the clear teaching of the Bible, and Christianity itself is often guilty of reshaping the Scriptures to better fit them to the passing opinions of the day. The Scriptures are understood to be far less than what the original writers intended. Even pastors and preachers can be hesitant to stand behind the absolute claims of the Bible. Yet we abandon the entire basis of Christianity when we no longer see the Bible as the absolute truth of God. A Christianity that no longer adheres to the Bible's position as absolute truth is no longer Christianity. The truth of Scripture is at the heart of everything the Christian believes, and to believe the Bible is to believe everything the Bible says.

The Bible makes clear and repeated claims that it is the source of absolute truth in the world. Peter stated that

"...no prophecy of the scripture is of any private interpretation. For the prophecy came not ⊡in old time by the will of man. but ⊡holy men of God spake as they were moved by the Holy Ghost." (2 Pet. 1.20)

If God is the author of the Scripture, then surely the Bible should be the absolute authority for our lives. Who has a greater claim on our lives than God? Whether we agree or disagree with them, whether we understand or misunderstand them, the words of God in the Bible form the written record of absolute truth in the world. Solomon said in Proverbs,

"Every □□word of God is □pure. □He is a □shield unto them that put their trust in him. □Add thou not unto his words, Lest he reprove thee, and thou □be found a liar." (Prov. 30.5).

The word pure in this passage means true. Solomon is claiming that every single word of God is true. We can only say this of God's word. No other writing is describable in this way. This means every word of God is true absolutely without qualification or exception.

In John's gospel, Jesus said, *"If ye continue in my word, then □are ye my disciples indeed; And ye shall know □the truth, and the truth □shall make you free." (Jn. 8.31-32)*. Note the definite article Jesus used in this verse. Jesus did not say if we abide in His word we will know *a* truth. He states that we will know *the* truth. There is a vast difference between the belief that the Bible is *the* truth, and belief that the Bible is merely *a* truth. In few places does secularism clash more violently with Christianity than in the arena of the absolute. You will be accepted if you use the indefinite article *a*, to describe your view of Scripture. When you remove the indefinite article *a*, and replace it with the definite article, *the*, however, little tolerance will come your way. The pressure

Christianity now faces is to back away from our stance that the Bible is the truth and represents absolute truth for all humanity.

Christians today must be ready to face this pressure. Speaking to the Apostles in Matthew chapter ten, Jesus said, "*Behold, I send you forth as sheep in the midst of wolves. be ye therefore wise as serpents, and harmless as doves.*" *(Mat. 10.16)*. The enemy is a master deceiver. If we are not prepared with the wisdom needed to spot his activity, we risk falling into the traps he sets. Few people desire to be viewed as unreasonable radicals who follow their religion blindly. They do not desire to offend people and prefer to live at peace with their neighbors and coworkers. But many of Satan's most effective traps come with the sign, "*This way to peace.*" It is entirely possible for the Christian to live at peace with those who do not share his belief in God. A Christian does not require another person to become Christian before they show them kindness, respect, and love. Jesus Himself told us to love even our enemies. Sadly though, this does not appear to be the case on the other side of the debate. The secular world insists that we abandon our long-held view of Scripture. Christians are considered a danger to society if they do not let go of their belief in the absolute truth of God's word. They are accused of hate speech when they share what the Bible says about men, women, and the family. None of this should be surprising to the student of Christian history. Most Christians martyred for their belief in God and His word were executed as law breakers. They were not considered heroes by the world. They were seen instead as criminals, as was their Lord at Calvary.

The Lost Anchor

∞

We will not be required to abandon our belief in the Bible for *ourselves*. Instead, we will be required to let go of our belief in the Bible as the absolute truth for *all*. Our preaching that the Bible is *the* truth, that Jesus is *the* way, will have to give way to preaching that asserts that the Bible is merely *a* truth, and Jesus is just one of many ways to Heaven. Satan will make this change sound like a most reasonable thing to do. Many professing Christians will put down their Bible's and wring their hands, hoping to avoid the persecution or disapproval of the world. They will hide behind the thought that they are just being wise and prudent. They will claim they are just being pragmatic; that it is better to go along to get along than to invite trouble into their comfortable lives. Yet to surrender this ground upon which all orthodox Christianity has stood since Christ is to surrender the entire struggle. There is no safe place of retreat for Christianity once we surrender the teaching that the Bible establishes absolute truth for all men. To relinquish this ground is to leave the Christian faith altogether.

It will be a god of our own imagination that we will serve when we cease holding to the doctrine that God's word is true without error or omission. It is here that the Christian faith makes its final stand. Our nation has already disconnected itself from its anchor and Satan would have all Christians do the same. We know that he will not be entirely successful. There will be faith on the earth when Jesus returns. Throughout history, God has preserved a remnant who have refused to surrender the Bible's place as the anchor of their lives, their homes, their churches, and their communities. Try as he might, the enemy will never overcome the witness of the bride of Christ on earth. Though all others abandon her, she will remain safely tied to God and His word. The warning cry made in this book then is not a cry of *desperation*. It is instead a cry of *invitation*. An invitation to each of us to commit to being a part of those who maintain their hold on the anchor of God's word. An invitation to a life of joy, peace, certainty, and meaning available to all who will bow in humility before God and live obediently to His word.

Chapter 4 - The Circular Argument

"But and if ye suffer for righteousness' sake, happy are ye, and be not afraid of their terror, neither be troubled; but sanctify the Lord God in your hearts, and be ready always to give an answer to every man that asketh you a reason of the hope that is in you with meekness and fear." (1 Peter 3:14–15)

Faith and Reason

"Says who?" Most of us have asked this question at some point. When given instructions by someone whose authority we do not recognize, we challenge the validity of the instructions. We do

not feel an obligation to obey commands given by those who are not in a recognized position of authority. No one teaches us to do this; it is an innate response to claims of authority, and the Bible is not immune from this scrutiny. Skeptics often raise questions like, *"Why should I believe the Bible is the source of absolute truth?"* and *"Where does the Bible get its authority to make the claims it makes?"* Feeling ill-equipped to answer, Christians often respond with calls for belief unaccompanied by reason. Belief in the Bible and in God depend on a faith the skeptic does not yet have. The writer of Hebrews tells us that *"without faith, it is impossible to please [God],"* *(Heb. 11.6)* so we cannot dismiss the requirement of faith in Christianity. We cannot reason our way into Christianity apart from faith, but neither is faith absent of reason. God created us with a mind *and* a heart. By doing so, He gave us the ability to *think* as well as *feel*. Christianity then must not run from sincere questions by arguing that reason and faith are mutually exclusive, just as the thinking unbeliever should not be encouraged to set aside his reason to find faith. This approach to evangelism has been a stumbling block for many who cannot get past what they see as reasonable objections to the Christian faith. When Christians avoid the rational questions of the skeptic, the response is usually more skepticism.

Evading the questions posed to Christianity can also lead to the substitution of emotional experiences for true conversion, when rather than engaging the thoughtful unbeliever and his questions, a misguided reliance on emotion unhinged from reason is suggested. But the Bible instructs us to be ready to give *reasons* for our belief. *(1 Pet. 3.15)*. Faith and reason, emotion and intellect, are not enemies, but are two parts of the complex whole that make up a human being. God is not interested in saving a *part* of our nature. He sent His Son to die in our place so we might love Him with all our heart, mind, soul, and strength. In a word, He wants us to love Him with all of ourselves. With these thoughts in view, I want to address a question that lies at the heart of why many refuse to believe the Bible.

The Circular Argument

One trained in logic will often recognize the Christian argument for the absolute truth of the Bible as circular, and thus an illegitimate, argument. Simply stated, a circular argument is an argument that ends where it begins. To say, "*Peter loves grapes because they are his favorite.*" is a circular argument. Skeptics of the Bible mark the fact that Christians use the premise of their argument as their conclusion and then dismiss Christianity's view of the Bible. If this sounds confusing, an example dialog between a Christian and a skeptic might help clear things up.

Christian. *"The Bible is the source of absolute truth."*

Skeptic. *"Why do you believe that? What proof do you have?"*

Christian. *"I believe the Bible is true absolutely because the Bible says it is."*

Skeptic. *"You can't just say that the Bible is true because the Bible says it is true. That's not proof. Your argument is circular."*

This back and forth can go on endlessly, and with no clear exit ramp, the discussion about the circular argument becomes its own circle.

Has the skeptic won the debate by asking a question the Christian could not answer? Should the Christian concede defeat, put his Bible down and leave his faith? To the contrary, there is no need to be intimidated or resort to a faith that replaces reason instead of compliments it. The skeptic has not disproven the Christian's argument. He has merely questioned the validity of the argument on the grounds that it is illegitimate due to its circular nature. There is a response that does not dismiss the requirement for faith, yet also provides a reasoned reply. The circular argument claim against the Bible is not as solid as you might think.

What then is the response to this circular argument accusation? Simple, *guilty.* You read that correctly. Christianity does use a circular argument when it claims that the Bible is true absolutely. When asked why we believe the Bible is true, we refer right back to the Bible, and that is undeniably a circular argument. However, before the believer raises the white flag of surrender and the unbeliever shouts in triumph, there is more to consider.

The Inevitability of the Circular Argument

The Lost Anchor

Arguments for absolute authority will inevitably involve circular arguments. Something must have the final word and serve as the final authority. Whatever that something is, its selection will involve circular reasoning. Wayne Grudem speaks to this topic in his *Systematic Theology*. Writing about the circular nature of all final authorities, Grudem calls out the following examples.

"My reason is my ultimate authority because it seems reasonable to me to make it so. Logical consistency is my ultimate authority because it is logical to make it so. The findings of human sensory experiences are the ultimate authority for discovering what is real and what is not, because our human senses have never discovered anything else. thus, human sense experience tells me that my principle is true. I know there can be no ultimate authority because I do not know of any such ultimate authority. "[3]

Grudem goes on to state, *"In all of these arguments for an ultimate standard of truth, an absolute authority for what to believe, there is an element of circularity involved. "*[4]

---

[3] Grudem, W. A. (2004). Systematic theology: an introduction to biblical doctrine (p. 79). Leicester, England; Grand Rapids, MI: Inter-Varsity Press; Zondervan Pub. House.

[4] Grudem, W. A. (2004). Systematic theology: an introduction to biblical doctrine (p. 79). Leicester, England; Grand Rapids, MI: Inter-Varsity Press; Zondervan Pub. House.

∞

It should be noted that the accusation that the Christian uses circular reasoning can be easily turned around on the skeptic. Referring to the earlier exchange between the Christian and the skeptic, one way for the Christian to respond is provided below.

Christian. *"I believe the Bible is the source of absolute truth."*

Skeptic. *"Why do you believe that? What proof do you have?"*

Christian. *"I believe the Bible is the source of absolute truth because the Bible says it is."*

Skeptic. *"You can't just say that the Bible is true because the Bible says it is true. What proof do you have that you are right about the Bible? Your argument is circular."*

Christian. *"Perhaps it is, but so is your objection. You say that the Bible must obey man's rules of logic because it is logical to you that this be true. But that too is circular, so both of our positions are logically equal."*

∞

Given the requirement of circular reasoning for any claim for absolute truth, the skeptics accusation against using it loses its power. How could a Christian argue for his belief in the Bible and *not* make a circular argument? What source of truth outside of Scripture should the believer provide that would convince the unbeliever of the Bible's authenticity? How can the Christian be true to his conviction that the Bible is the absolute truth and yet call upon something outside of the Bible to confirm that conviction? If you demand that the Christian prove the Bible is true according to science, would his belief not ultimately be in science and not the Bible? If you require the Christian to present documented historical proof for the Bible, would not his conviction be based on the accuracy and validity of recorded history, and not the Scriptures? The reason the Christian cannot provide external proof of the Bible's place as the source of absolute truth is because he is presenting to you his belief in the *absolute*. Absolute truth must not rely upon anything outside of itself, or it is no longer absolute truth, but simply one truth among many. What the believer cannot do, is place his faith partially in the Bible, and partially in some other corroborating source, be that source science, history, or the mere opinions of others. To do so would be to contradict the essential claims of the Scripture. If the Bible depends on any other source to validate itself, then it is not the single source of absolute truth which it claims to be.

The accusation of using a circular argument presents a difficulty for the Christian on the surface, but the lack of an answer is perfectly reasonable after careful consideration because the question itself rejects the claims of Scripture. The issue then is not an issue of reason, but faith, since the believers' position is just as reasonable as the unbelievers. The great irony that is often buried beneath the surface of this entire discussion is that faith is required on both sides of the argument. Neither can claim their position without exercising faith in their chosen absolute.

The question then is not whether we are guilty of circular reasoning when selecting what ultimately guides our lives. The question instead becomes *what* have we chosen as our final authority? One thing lies at the heart of all your decisions. Something guides you as you raise your children, love your spouse, and work for your boss. Something guides you when you decide what books to read, what shows to watch, and what to do with your leisure time. Something guides you even as you consider what should guide you. What is the final authority in your life? Is it your intellect and what it believes to be true? Is it your heart and what it feels is true? Perhaps it is time to recognize that your understanding is limited, and your feelings have been in the past, and can be again in the future, changeable, malleable, even wrong.

Something is sitting in the driver's seat for your decisions. Whatever that something is, its selection involves circular reasoning. You cannot avoid the circular argument for the determination of absolute truth and final authority.

Chapter 5 - The Call to Return to Scripture

"Now therefore fear the Lord, and serve him in sincerity and in truth. and put away the gods which your fathers served on the other side of the flood, and in Egypt; and serve ye the Lord. And if it seem evil unto you to serve the Lord, choose you this day whom ye will serve; whether the gods which your fathers served that were on the other side of the flood, or the gods of the Amorites, in whose land ye dwell. but as for me and my house, we will serve the Lord." (Joshua 24:14–15)

Christianity at a Crossroads

America has been moving away from God at a steady pace, and many who maintain a Biblical worldview no longer recognize their own nation. Christianity is at a crossroad with only two choices before it. The path of acceptance in society, which now requires the modification of the core claims of the Bible, or the path that leads back to the historical conviction that God's word is the standard of truth for all men. Sadly, it appears that a considerable number standing under the banner of Christianity have already chosen the first path. Unwilling to risk rejection by society or a reduction in attendance, they have backed away from the clear teaching of the Bible. Desiring to sound like the world so they do not offend the world, they now spend more time apologizing for the Bible than they do proclaiming its message. Like Eve in the Garden, Christianity is confronted with Satan's efforts to deny and remove God's word from our minds and hearts. Many have already eaten this forbidden fruit and death has followed just as surely as it did for our first parents. One Christian denomination after another has backed away from God's word and are now empty shells of what they once were. Though churches still dot our land, it is of little comfort when we remember that outward expressions of Christianity often continue long after the day when true inward Christianity has been left behind. Church buildings, programs, budgets, staff, and weekend services typically survive many years after the Spirit of God has departed the scene. It is time now for Christians to take a hard and honest look at their church and their own views. Questions must be asked, and answers sincerely sought. Is the Bible the central source of truth in my church? Do I learn how to parent my children from the

Bible? If someone removed all our Bibles on Monday morning, would it be Sunday before any of us even noticed? Does the pastor spend his time exposing his people to God's word, or does he spend most of his time talking about the latest Christian fad? What do my children really think of the issues of homosexuality and marriage? Do they read the Bible at all? Do I really think the church is effectively countering the indoctrination my children receive from the secular world with a few minutes on Sunday morning?

Honest answers to these questions reveal the dire state of Christianity in America. The anchor of God's word no longer holds our nation, and the church is feeling the pull of the world to let it go as well. What Christianity does with the Bible today will determine our path ahead. We can reset and tighten our grip once again on the anchor of the Bible, or we can let it slip from our grasp and cling instead to the world. Holding to the Bible is the path that leads to life and blessing. Letting it go leads to chaos, fear, and death.

The more we know about the Bible, the greater the likelihood is that we will make right choices in our lives. One reason for the loosened grip on the word of God is the significant ignorance that now exists concerning the Bible itself. An unspoken fear within the walls of many churches is that the Bible cannot stand up to scrutiny, and we therefore do not undertake a close look at the

Bible. Yet the skeptic of the Bible is like a boy throwing pebbles at a granite wall with foundations deep in the earth. Throw as hard as he can for as long as he desires, the wall will remain unmoved, unchanged, and as solid as ever. Alfred Edersheim speaks to this in his book, *Bible History Old Testament*. Edersheim writes,

"...the more deep, calm, and careful our study [of the Bible], the more ample the evidence it will bring to light to confirm our faith against all attacks of the enemy[5]*"*

All the pebbles of doubt thrown against the Bible fall harmlessly to the ground when we make a *deep*, *calm*, and *careful* study of the Bible (*Mat. 24.35*). In the following chapters I will make a brief examination of several fundamental truths regarding the Bible. Truths that I believe will tighten our grip on the anchor of the Bible in our lives.

Is Faith Blind?

Before moving on to the specific doctrines addressed in this book, it will be important for us to understand the part faith plays

---

[5] Edersheim, A. (1975). Bible History: Old Testament (Vol. 1, p.13). Grand Rapids, MI: William B. Eerdmans Publishing Company.

in our examination. Certain questions can be helpful to frame the balance between faith and reason regarding the truth of Scripture. Can we make reasoned arguments for the Bible's claims or do we accept them as a matter of faith only? How do we know that the Bible is true? Is there evidence for us to weigh or do we believe the Bible based on blind faith alone? Do Christians even have a responsibility to provide reasoned arguments for their claims regarding the Bible, or is it enough to say that the Bible's claims are accepted as a matter of faith?

Those who possess true faith understand that only the unbeliever speaks of faith as being blind. Faith is not blind. Faith is not a substitute for knowledge. It is the key that unlocks true knowledge. Faith is like light. You do not see light, but you see what the light reveals. Light then is a *means* to sight, even though we do not actually *see* the light. Faith acts in the same way in that it is the *means* to knowledge. And by this I do not mean *mystical* knowledge. I mean hard facts and observable truths. Faith makes plain what is right in front of us. Faith opens the eyes to see what is already there. Faith does not invent realities that did not already exist. Rather, faith opens our eyes to see in such a way that we are utterly stunned by our previous blindness. The Bible uses words like *evidence* and *substance* when referring to faith *(Heb. 11.1)*. Yet many consider faith more akin to a whim, a fancy, or an uncertain hope.

A primary reason for this misunderstanding of faith is the influence of materialism. Dressed in the lab coat of the scientist, the materialist tells us that if something is observable or measurable in the physical world, then it is real. If something is said to be unobservable to human observation, or immeasurable by human standards, then it is not real. The conclusion that follows this hypothesis is that because faith cannot be measured or observed, it is therefore not real. To believe something based on faith is to believe it blindly according to a growing number of people today. The supreme rule and standard of knowledge has become what science can see and measure. Said another way, if the scientist cannot prove that a thing exists, or that an idea is true, then that thing or idea can only be believed with blind faith.

Many atheists attempt to sound as though they are only being reasonable when they insist on hard evidence before they will believe something is real. But surely, we can all see the weakness in this logic. The claim is essentially this, that unless our *present understanding* of science can account for a thing, then that thing must not exist. Yet science itself is always changing its opinion and adjusting its catalog of truth as new knowledge comes to light. Before science had advanced to the point of discovering that the earth was round, was the earth flat? Before the invention of the microscope, were germs, viruses, and bacteria nonexistent? Did they not exist prior to our being able to see them? Is reality determined merely by our ability to measure and observe it? This line of thinking does not hold up even in the physical world, and yet many people cling to this flawed logic with reference to the Bible and the spiritual world. They make the argument that there is no way to observe the truths claimed by the Bible, and thus the Bible cannot be objectively true. The problem we are dealing with, however, is not a problem with the state of truth itself, but with the measurements and tools by which we establish what is true. And science is simply the wrong tool to validate the truth of the Bible.

A sociology professor once told me I could not know God was real because I could not observe Him. I responded by telling him that his statement depended entirely on how one defined the word *observe*. I shared that I had observed God many times. I could not put that observation in a test tube to undergo a scientific examination, but I had observed Him. Of that I was certain.

This is not to say that science is an unnecessary or unhelpful field of study. The Christian should not shy away from any of the varied fields of scientific discovery. When rightly undertaken science involves the methodical unwrapping of the unimaginable complexity of the world God called forth out of nothing. The right end of science is the right end of all things, which is the glory of God.

The simple point I wish to make here is that we must let go of any concerns that science will be our enemy and blind faith our ally as we approach the study of the various doctrines related to the Bible. As we will see, there is much evidence and substance that lies underneath the claims of the Bible. It is to every Christian's advantage to know this evidence and be ready to counter the attacks of the skeptics in academia, popular culture, the media, and politics. Further and more importantly, Christians are commanded by God to always be ready to give a *reason* for their *faith (1 Pet. 3.15)*. And there it is, the marriage of reason and faith in the word of God. Faith, apart from reason is a fairy tale meant for children. Yet, reason apart from faith is the path of the arrogant fool who does not admit that his knowledge is limited by his own limitations. The following chapters will look at several specific doctrines about the Bible. I will provide evidence that supports these doctrines, but I do not provide evidence to argue anyone into a simple intellectual agreement with the Christian faith. I provide it hoping it will serve as kindling for a fire of faith that will set hearts ablaze, providing the light (knowledge) and warmth (faith) necessary to rightly understand these essential doctrines of the Christian faith.

A Word of Encouragement

In twenty-seven years of ministry, I have found the Bible to be precisely what it claims to be. I have not uncovered difficulties that cast doubt on the place of God's word in my life and the life of the world. I have shared the gospel in Europe, Africa, Asia, and many places in the United States. The people, culture, and languages differed from one place to another. The political, economic, and societal challenges were unique to each. What remained the same was the applicability and truthfulness of the word of God. You can trust the Bible. You can trust it because you can trust God. Some hesitate to investigate the core doctrines of Christianity out of fear that they will discover something that might cast doubt on their faith, and this fear often leads to the avoidance of diligent study and thoughtful consideration of the fundamental tenets of the faith of Christianity. We must understand though that God made us thinking and rational creatures as well as emotional and feeling creatures.

God made a complete man when He formed Adam and gave Him life. Adam was whole in body, soul, spirit, and mind. The greatest commandment God has given to man is that we love Him with all our heart, soul, mind, and strength. It follows then that to give God what He has commanded us to give, we must give Him not only a *sincere heart*, but a *disciplined and prepared mind*. The attempt to separate the mind and heart of man represents an attempt to separate what God intended to be individual parts of a whole.

What follows in this book are truths about the Scripture regarding some of the boldest claims of Christianity. Claims that the Bible is unique among all other books. That it was authored by God. That God watched over the specific selection of the sixty-six books that comprise the Bible. That the Bible is inerrant, necessary, clear, and sufficient. When these truths are understood and believed with both the mind and the heart, it will strengthen our hold on the historical anchor of the Bible. We will be better able to hold onto this anchor when the world attempts to pry it from our hands. Rather than drift aimlessly through our lives with nothing to hold us secure, we will live with a meaning and purpose only possible when absolute truth is known. Instead of stumbling around in the darkness in a world that denies truth, we will live in the light of God's word, the lamp to our feet and the light to our path. Thus, knowing where we are, and where we are going, we can proceed with confidence and not fear. May God make this true in each of our lives.

Part Two

Recognizing the Anchor

Chapter 6 - The Uniqueness of Scripture

"There is no one like You among the gods, O Lord, Nor are there any works like Yours." Psalm 86:8

Introduction to Part Two

In Part One, I focused on the lost anchor of the Bible in our nation and called attention to the fact that our nation is no longer guided by Scripture. Sadly, this is also true within many Christian circles. While there have been, and there will likely continue to be, occasional references made to the Scriptures during times of crisis and difficulty, the day-to-day activity of the average man on the street includes no time at all with the Bible. Even many Christians open their bibles for only a few short minutes when the preacher reads his text on Sunday. This has been the case for so long that many have forgotten what the anchor looks like, and many others have never truly seen it for themselves. There is no longer an understanding of the fundamental doctrines of the Christian faith as they relate to the Scripture. Part Three of this book will address how we might restore the lost anchor, but before we can restore the anchor, we must recognize it when we see it.

My aim in part two is to provide a review of the core doctrines that orthodox Christianity has historically held about the Bible. Many others far more able than myself have written about these doctrines in much greater depth and I do not intend to compete with them. Yet, I hope to address these subjects in such a way as to make them approachable to anyone who desires to understand them. I am not writing primarily for the seminary student, academic, or the preacher, though I hope they too will read this book. It might be that in desiring to go beyond the basics of the faith, the basics themselves become lost. At no point, however, do the basic doctrines of Christianity become unnecessary. All that we understand from the Bible must be understood in light of the core doctrines of the Scripture. To move beyond them would be to depart from the well-worn path of the historical view of God's word. We pave a path of our own making when we step off the path of historical and Biblical Christianity. Yet men often like to strike out in new directions. Preachers can be guilty of thinking they have some new revelation, or some nuance of faith that will entice their hearers. But Solomon said there is nothing new under the sun. *(Ecc. 1.9)*. We should remember that this truth applies to our sermons as well. It would be difficult to estimate the number of sermons that have been delivered throughout history by tens of thousands of preachers. We must not think that in our few decades of ministry we will stumble onto some new thought which no one before us has ever considered or brought out from the Bible. We are reminded that all new news is just old news happening to new people. Yet men like to hear new things. They gravitate toward those who claim to have a new revelation from God, but the path of new revelation never leads to life; it leads to death. There is a reason that the path of historical Christianity is well worn. When walked to its completion it leads to Heaven. Our task is to marvel at the path already given and apply ourselves to walking in that path every day. Do not be led astray by those who claim that they have a new word from God that departs from the clear teaching of the Bible. All such paths are simply different lanes on the broad road that leads to destruction.

In the following chapters, I will address the following doctrines.

1. The Uniqueness of Scripture
2. The Doctrine of Scripture
3. The Authorship of Scripture
4. The Authority of Scripture
5. The Selection of Scripture
6. The Inerrancy of Scripture
7. The Necessity of Scripture
8. The Sufficiency of Scripture

9. The Clarity of Scripture

These doctrines reveal what the Bible says about itself. We do not believe the Bible in any true sense when we do not believe what it says about itself. To say that we believe the Bible without believing what it says about itself is to say that we believe a man's testimony about others when he is known to lie about himself.

The doctrines addressed in this book do not form an exhaustive list, but I believe they represent the core attributes of the Bible; the anchor that we must restore in our lives. We cannot claim a secure connection to the anchor of God's word if we do not believe that the Bible is inerrant. We have become separated from the anchor when we no longer recognize the authority of God's word over our lives and over the church. Many professing Christians claim a connection to the anchor yet deny one or more of these foundational doctrines. Where this is true, the Bible is not the anchor. Some other anchor is chosen instead; an anchor that will not hold in the storms of this life or the next.

The following chapters are an attempt to focus the reader on the true anchor. To see it for what it is, and not for what the world claims it to be. To get a glimpse of the truths of the greatest book ever written. When rightly understood, these doctrines will not lead to academic advancement only. They will drive a person to their knees in humble thanksgiving to God for giving us such an anchor to hold us firmly in His presence. Theology, when rightly studied, leads to worship. Where there is no worship, there is no proper theology. Yet, where there is no right theology, there is also no true worship. Worship and theology must be linked together. Throw away theology and you will soon worship a god of your own making. Toss out worship, and you will soon become a valley of dry bones with perhaps the skeletal remains of life, but no true life. May our study of these doctrines be theologically accurate, yet infused throughout with true and sincere worship of God.

The Unique Message of the Scripture

The central message of the Bible is unique among all other sacred religious texts. Many people claim that all religions are the same, but even a casual reading of the Bible reveals this to be false. The Bible alone speaks of what God has done for man instead of what man must do for God. In Buddhism, the message is that a man must empty himself of passion, aversion, and ignorance. In Hinduism, one must live a good enough life to be reborn to a greater life. In Islam, the five daily prayers must be spoken, and the dietary restrictions observed. Acknowledging that much more could be said of the religions of Buddhism, Hinduism, and Islam, the point made here is that within each of these religions, the message is about what man must do to appease God, but this is not the message of Christianity. Christianity presents a message about what God has done to make it possible for man to be made right with Him. In man-made religion, the focus is on the activity, worth, and merit of man. In Christianity, the focus is on the activity, worth, and merit of God.

The Lost Anchor

In the opening chapters of the Bible God tells us of His work in creation. From nothing God created everything when He spoke the universe into existence during the creation week as recorded in Genesis chapters one and two. The opening line of the Bible reads, *"In the beginning God created the heavens and the earth." (Gen. 1.1).* The raw materials of the universe came into existence in that singular moment. God continued to shape, separate, and identify specific parts of creation over the next six days, but in verse one, from nothing God created everything. During the creation week, light shined into the darkness. The sun, moon, and stars took their places in the heavens. Flowers, plants, and trees covered the ground. Mountains rose and valleys fell. The sea was filled with countless creatures, some of whom we are still discovering today. The sights and sounds of the birds in the sky were seen and heard for the first time. The world was shaped and prepared with a precision only possible for God. One of the reasons men are so nervous about the climate and the earth, is that we intuitively know that its complexity is far beyond his ability to comprehend, much less control. As the closing and crowning act of His creation, God created man. God did not bring man into a formless, empty, and dark world. Instead, He brought man into a fully formed world specifically designed for human beings. God was working for us before we drew our first breath in the world. No other sacred texts speak of God in this way.

The message of God's working on man's behalf before he was born is repeated throughout Scripture and we quickly discover that the Bible is telling a far different story than does Buddha, Allah, or any of the 330 million Hindu gods.

60

Before I formed thee in the belly I knew thee; and before thou camest forth out of the womb I sanctified thee, and I ordained thee a prophet unto the nations." (Jer. 1.5)

"I was cast upon thee from the womb. Thou art my God from my mother's belly." (Ps. 22.10)

"Listen, O isles, unto me; And hearken, ye people, from far; The Lord hath called me from the womb; From the bowels of my mother hath he made mention of my name." (Isa. 49.1)

"But when it pleased God, who separated me from my mother's womb, and called me by his grace," (Gal. 1.15)

The most striking work God performed on our behalf before any of us were born was His work to make salvation possible. Salvation is not dependent on us, and only the Bible speaks about what God has done to accomplish the work of salvation for fallen man. Genesis chapter three records the dark day when sin entered the world through man's disobedience. Falling to Satan's deception, Eve ate the forbidden fruit of the tree of the knowledge of good and evil. Adam then ate as well, and humanity was plunged into sin and became separated from God. It is at this point that the Bible begins to tell a different story from that of the other major religions in the world. Rather than record what man did to regain his place before God, the Bible unfolds the story of what God had already done to redeem fallen man.

Man is not the hero in the Bible. Many people are under the false impression that the Bible records the stories of righteous men and women who lived such pious lives that they merited entrance into heaven when they died. As a result, many see Christianity as a religion that teaches the need for us to live a moral life to be saved. The concept behind this distorted view of Christianity is that so long as our good deeds outweigh our bad, we will be saved. This view however is not a Biblical one. The Bible shows that all men are sinners, and even the heroes of the Bible are shown to be imperfect. Abraham is revealed to be a liar. King David an adulterer and murderer. Peter is seen denying Christ with a curse.

The Bible tells us plainly that there is nothing a man could do to buy back his position before God. Paul told the Galatians,

"...a man is not justified by the works of the law, but by the faith of Jesus Christ, even we have believed in Jesus Christ, that we might be justified by the faith of Christ, and not by the works of the law. for by the works of the law shall no flesh be justified." (Gal. 2.16).

Paul reminds the Ephesians of the same truth when he tells them, *"For by grace are ye saved through faith; and that not of yourselves. it is the gift of God. Not of works, lest any man should boast." (Eph. 2.8-9).* Time and again the Bible presents us with the truth that salvation is a work of God on behalf of man. Salvation is not a reward for good behavior. Salvation is the ultimate manifestation of the grace and mercy of a kind, loving, and benevolent God.

A careful examination of Genesis chapter three reveals this to be the case. We do not read that Adam and Eve came to their senses and said to one another, "*We have to go to God and make this right!*" when they introduced sin into the world. We do not see them sacrificing an animal. They do not run to God and ask for forgiveness. In fact, we do not see them approach God at all. Busy sowing together fig leaves to hide their nakedness, they made no attempt to seek God. However, God sought them even as they tried to avoid Him. God called out to Adam and asked, "*Where art thou?*" *(Gen. 3.9)*. It is difficult to overstate the striking difference this represents between the Bible and the books of the other major religions of the world. Rather than tell glowing tales of man's worthy and valiant efforts to find God, the Bible speaks about what God did to find a lost and helpless humanity, who were doing their best to hide behind bushes and fig leaves. We can only say with Paul, "*Thanks be unto God for His unspeakable gift!*" *(2 Cor. 9:15)* If ever theology and worship should come together, surely it is here.

God knew precisely where Adam was when He called out to him on that day. He had created the very bush behind which Adam was hiding. God did not ask this question for His own benefit, He asked it so that Adam would consider the answer to the question and contemplate his newfound separation. Adam's name literally means, "*man*". When God called out to Adam, then, He was in one sense calling out to us all. He called out to Abraham, to Joseph, to David, to the Apostles, and the many others we read about in the Bible. He calls out to you and me as well when He says, "*Where art thou?*" His purpose is the same as it was for the first Adam (man). That purpose is so we might realize our separation from Him. That we would see our sin and our need for a savior. The entire Bible is the story of God calling out to man, and of what He has done to make salvation possible, and it reveals the complete inability of man to make himself righteous before God based on his own works. This central truth and message of the Bible makes it unique among all other writings of the religions of the world.

Detached from the anchor of the Bible, false religion is empty and deeply manipulative. It is empty because it does not stand to reason to think that God needs anything from man. God's independence is such that He does not need man to complete something within Himself. He did not create the world from a place of need or emptiness in Himself. In eternity before the world began, God was complete as Father, Son, and Spirit. Within the Trinity there was perfect, complete, and fulfilling love and fellowship. It was not as though God was lonely, and in His loneliness, He created man. It is silly to think we could do anything to so impress God that He would offer us a place in heaven. Yet the manipulative tactic of many false religions is to coerce a man into certain behaviors they are told will please God. But what can you or I ever do to impress the One who set the sun in its place? What work can we perform that would amaze God? The Bible, like no other writing, makes these truths plain.

Kent Welch

Chapter 7 - The Doctrine of Scripture

"As David's time to die drew near, he charged Solomon his son, saying, "I am going the way of all the earth. Be strong, therefore, and show yourself a man. "Keep the charge of the LORD your God, to walk in His ways, to keep His statutes, His commandments, His ordinances, and His testimonies, according to what is written in the Law of Moses, that you may succeed in all that you do and wherever you turn," 1 Kings 2:1–3

Scripture and Specific Truth

The steady erosion of the absolute in our society has directly affected the way many Christians view the Bible. Many fly what they believe to be a flag of peace with the world by denying the absolute truth claimed by the Scripture, but as is always the case when attempting to compromise with the world, a flag of surrender ends up being flown. The world will not assail a professing Christian who denies that the Bible is the absolute truth. This leads many to believe they are at peace with the world, and they convince themselves they can hold to their Christianity while living at peace with a world that denies everything Christianity claims to be true. But they are not at peace. It is much more probable that they are spiritually dead or weakened to such a point that the enemy sees no further need to attack. Satan will not bother a cultural Christian who does not truly believe in Christ. Why would Satan provoke a professing Christian who does not in truth believe God? What does he stand to gain? Satan directs his efforts instead at those who believe Jesus with all their heart, and those who see in the Bible the absolute rule of life God has given to men. This is the Christian who will find persecution for their belief, but the presence of this persecution in our lives should not concern us nearly as much as its absence. Paul warned Timothy that, "... *all that will live godly in Christ Jesus shall suffer persecution." (2 Tim. 3.12)*. If we do not experience persecution in our lives, then we must conclude by Paul's words that our lives are not as godly as they ought to be.

It is to our advantage to recognize the forms of attack that will come against us as it relates to belief in the Bible. A frequent attack comes in the form of denying the *specific*, while allowing for the *general*, *situational*, or *relative*. As the late well-known Christian Apologist Ravi Zacharias was fond of saying, *the faith of many people suffers the death of a thousand qualifications*. The inescapable truth though, is that the Bible makes *specific, clear,* and *directed* commands for men to follow. The Bible is a book of doctrine. It is not a book that contains a few good ideas for us to consider. The Bible is not a book from which we can pick what we like and discard what we do not. God did not give Israel tablets of stone that contained *The Ten Suggestions*. Despite this, the specific doctrines of the Bible are often replaced with a general Christian ethic. Here, like perhaps nowhere else, the devil is in the details.

Jesus gives us a view into the importance of the specific nature of Scripture when He said that "*Till heaven and earth pass, one jot or one tittle shall in no wise pass from the law, till all be fulfilled.*" *(Mat. 5.18)* If every *i* will be dotted, and every *t* will be crossed, then every *i* and every *t* must have great significance. If even the smallest marks on individual letters in the Law are significant, then surely every command of God is of great significance as well.

God did not waste words in the Bible. He did not wax eloquent for the sake of eloquence. What God can say in just a few words has often amazed me. A single phrase of Scripture has the power to change our lives. Three words Jesus spoke in the Sermon on the Mount make this clear. Jesus told His followers to "*Love your enemies*". *(Mat. 5.44)*. Obedience to this one command would make you markedly different from most of the world. The world loves those that love them, but the Christian loves even those who hate them, speak ill of them, persecute them, or kill them. Many Christian martyrs in history shared the gospel with their executioners and forgave them for what they did. Stephen called out to God as the Jews stoned him and said, "*Lord, lay not this sin to their charge*". *(Acts 7.60)* The witness of these believers in Christ would not have been present nearly as powerfully if they had not obeyed the specific command of God to love their enemies. If they had turned the specific command of God to love their enemies into a general command to show them kindness, their witness would have suffered significantly. It is one thing to show kindness to an enemy. It is quite another to love them.

The Christian who views the Bible as God's specific call upon their life is a Christian prepared to live a life God will use, but the Christian who sees the Bible as merely a general set of guidelines will suffer in their walk with God. This might sound extreme but consider what is being said by the Christian who speaks of God's word as merely a set of guiding principles. They are saying to God, "*I believe your word to a point Lord, but surely you do not mean for me to live a life so very different from the world around me.*" Excuses abound for viewing the Bible this way. Many claim that we live in a time when it is impossible to live by the specific commands of God. Viewing the Bible in this way makes God frivolous at best, and dishonest at worst.

Christians often lament that God does not appear to work in any specific way in their lives. They desire to see God do great things for them, and for those they love. They believe God to a point, but they do not see His specific hand of Providence in their lives. In many such cases, the root of the problem lies in the way they view and apply the Scripture to their lives. God's *specific work* in our lives is tied to our *specific obedience* to His *specific commands*. This is not to say that our obedience merits God's blessing or obligates Him in any way, but it is important to realize that the law of cause and effect is in operation. If we do not strive to obey God's specific commands, how can we expect to receive His specific blessings? If we do not actually and specifically repent of our sin, how can we expect to receive His forgiveness? If we are not actually meek, how can we expect to inherit the earth?

Christianity Devoid of Doctrine

To claim a belief in the Bible has historically been descriptive of the beliefs a person holds. To be a Christian was to be a follower of Jesus Christ, and an observer of the doctrines He taught. However, the descriptiveness of the word *Christian* has eroded over the centuries since Christ walked upon the earth. Regrettably, and to the detriment of Christianity and the world at large, claiming to be a Christian does not provide the clarity that it once did. In his book, *Baptist Church Manual*, J.M. Pendleton wrote,

"To say that [one believes] the Scriptures is to say nothing to the purpose. All will say this, and yet all differ as to the teachings of the Bible. There must be some distinctive declaration. What a man believes the Bible to teach is his creed, either written or unwritten.[6]*"*.

There is broad diversity within Christianity today regarding what the Bible teaches. Some differences of opinion are to be expected. In the right place, these differences can provide a healthy dissonance to challenge wrong ideas that might take root. Ideas which are not tied to the Bible, but to the traditions of men. We will treat this subject more fully in a later chapter. My purpose here is to call out the great lack of distinctiveness within Christianity today.

The response to this disparity of belief in many churches is to follow the approach, "*If you can't beat them, join them*". A Christianity *devoid* of doctrine is adopted instead of a Christianity *defined* by the doctrines of the Bible. Success is often measured by the numbers of people in the pew so churches often avoid areas of specific doctrine that would scatter the crowd. Words that sound spiritually enlightened are often spoken in defense of this approach. In churches across the country, you can hear phrases like the following:

- *"We just want everyone to feel welcome."*
- *"We don't want to offend anyone.*
- *"We just want to love people."*
- *"We don't want to get bogged down with Bible study and doctrine; we just want to praise Jesus."*

---

[6]Pendleton, J.M. (1966) Baptist Church Manual Revised (p.42). Nashville; Broadman Press

- *"We don't judge here; we accept people for who they are."*

While these thoughts sound good to ears well trained in political correctness, they can be deceptive words if we are not careful to discern what is behind them. We certainly want people to feel welcome in our churches, but the fact of the matter is that not everyone will feel welcome when God's word is spoken. We must look no further than how the Apostles and the Lord Himself were treated when they spoke the words of God to see the truth of this. People will be offended when the Gospel is presented. It is an inevitability. We should always seek to ensure the *messenger* is not offensive, but the *message* of the Bible offends those who are lost in their pride and denial of their need for God.

Jesus gathered massive crowds of people in the first year of His earthly ministry. Luke referred to these crowds when he wrote,

"And [Jesus] came down with them, and stood in the plain, and the company of his disciples, and a great multitude of people out of all Judaea and Jerusalem, and from the sea coast of Tyre and Sidon, which came to hear him, and to be healed of their diseases;" (Lk. 6.17).

People came to Jesus by the thousands. Within these multitudes, there were many varied opinions regarding right and wrong. Truth and error. The path to Heaven, and the path to Hell. Did Jesus adopt an approach that would be certain to welcome everyone? Was His primary concern that He not offend the crowd? Was He primarily focused on ensuring everyone felt accepted?

Did He want them to *like Him* more than He desired for them to *believe Him*? Was He willing to settle for being man's *popular friend*, rather than being their *outcast savior*? Did he manage and soften His message when the crowds began to scatter? Did He moderate His views on specific doctrine to appeal to a larger base?

The answer to all these questions is no. His insistence on presenting the exclusive message of the Gospel only grew as the crowds grew. If there had been church growth counselors present in Jesus' day, they would have been highly disappointed in His approach. We can almost see them cringing as Jesus' words and actions began to scatter the crowds. We know however that Jesus was not interested in being popular. He was not interested in wearing an earthly crown because His mission was to bear an earthly cross and die for the sins of the world so that through Him, the world might be saved. The mission of the church is the proclamation of this same exclusive and specific message. Her mission is not to be impressive to the world. The crowds will treat the church in the same manner as they treated her Lord. The few will find the narrow way to Christ while the majority will scatter and walk the broad way to destruction. *(Mat. 7.13-14)*. The Great Commission the Lord gave His church was not to assemble great crowds. It was to scatter and share with the whole world the specific doctrines He had taught. *(Mat. 28.19-20)*.

The temptation to moderate the message of Christ grows as the size and reach of a church grows. Satan convinces well intended Christians that the most important thing is that the church is growing in number. He encourages the preacher to drink the poisonous cup of pride by believing that his preaching is responsible for the large numbers that attend his church. More buildings are built; more programs are begun; more staff are hired. The budget grows and before long the church finds itself in a financial situation that demands the continued support of the crowd. When the inevitable choice between the support of the crowd and the preaching of the specific doctrines of Scripture emerges, all too many choose the crowd instead of Christ. Churches then distance themselves from the specific doctrines of Scripture. They present a Christ not found in Scripture. They moderate the message to appease the conscience of fallen men and women. Rather than encourage people to face the fact of their lostness and need of Christ, they provide them with a remedy that never truly takes away the pain, penalty, and guilt of sin. Walking hand in hand with the false prophets of the Old Testament, they heal the hurt of the people only lightly and proclaim *"Peace, Peace, when there is no peace." (Jer. 6.14, 8.11)*.

One of the most striking truths of the New Testament's account of the life of Christ is that so few followed Him. Jesus was the Son of God among men. He gave sight to the blind. His slightest touch or spoken word could heal the sick. The dead obeyed His voice and came forth from the grave. He taught with a power and authority like no other before Him. He was Immanuel, God among men. If men were the authors of Scripture, they would not have written the Gospel accounts of the life of Christ as they were. Human authors would have written that Jesus accepted the crowds' desire to make Him king. In a vision straight from Hollywood, Jesus would have entered Jerusalem on a white stallion at the head of a vast and powerful army. Certainly, His coming to Jerusalem the final time would not have been on a borrowed donkey, with only a few unimpressive followers, a mere few days before being crucified. Had men written the Gospel, we would read that Jesus' followers stood up against the Roman soldiers as they beat Him. Unable to endure the sight of their Lord's suffering and shame, they all would have attempted to save Him even if it cost them their lives.

Instead, the story of the Gospel is that Jesus went to the cross alone. The crowds had long since rejected Him and even His closest friends scattered in the final hours. With a curse, Peter denied he even knew the Lord. Instead of cheers of support and worship from the crowds, Jesus heard the united shouts of the people as they cried, "*Crucify*!" These truths baffle the mind and defy explanation outside of divine revelation. How could the world treat the Son of God this way? How could it be that no one stood with Him on the day of His crucifixion? How was it possible that a man who had done so much good for others would Himself be beaten within an inch of His life, stripped naked, spit upon, mocked, nailed to a cross and murdered in plain sight? We know of course that God was at work in all these things. I do not deny God's sovereign activity in the death of His only Son. Yet, I also see that Jesus' rejection was due to man's rejection of the specific message Jesus preached. Jesus claimed to be *the* light, *the* truth, *the* way. He claimed that apart from Him, no one could know God.

He taught God's specific (and exclusive) word to the world, and the world rejected Him for it. Had Jesus moderated His message, had He only substituted the specific truth of God with the relative truth of man, He would not have ended up on the cross. But had Jesus not ended up on the cross, you and I could never end up in Heaven.

The same eternal realities are at stake for the church. Namely, the eternal souls of men and women and the glory of our risen Lord. The church must choose between a desire to be true to God and seek His pleasure or seek the pleasure and acceptance of men. When the church ignores the specific doctrines of Scripture in favor of a message that dismisses them, they have chosen the crowd and rejected Christ. And in their fear of men, they never learn a right fear of God. It is important to remember that the Bible is not a book that merely provides guiding principles. It is a book that teaches specific doctrines. These specific doctrines will be the target of the enemy because he knows that the further we travel from the specific teaching of the Bible, the further we drift from our anchor, and the closer we get to following our own ideas, opinions, and traditions.

There is a sad irony when the specific doctrines of the Bible are rejected in favor of a less specific stance on its teaching. Many believe that being less offensive will lead to greater unity. This mistaken logic asserts that if the church would just moderate her tone on the issues of sin and be more accepting of the moral judgments of society, people will feel more unity and there will be less strife. This mistaken logic represents one of Satan's best laid traps for the church. It sounds like a perfectly rational and reasonable conclusion. If the church would be less judgmental, then more people would feel welcome and greater unity among the people would result. If the church would let go of her view of the Bible as the supreme standard by which all things should be judged, and adopt a position that allows for individuals to determine for themselves what applies to them, then we would all join hands and find our own paths to God. Though this might sound like a great plan that would attract great crowds of people to the church, the reality of this approach is far from unifying. When the standard of God's word is replaced with the opinions of men, you do not end up with a recipe for peace and agreement. You end up instead with a far more controversial, divisive, and hurtful environment than a commitment to God's word has ever produced. When God's word is the shared standard among a people, there is a source of truth by which they can successfully handle all doctrinal and relational difficulties. This leads to a unity not possible when the standard and arbiter of truth is nothing more substantial than one man's opinion versus another. Unity is not defined by the complete absence of strife or differences of opinion. Unity exists when everyone is looking to the same source to navigate those times of disagreement to a successful conclusion. A conclusion that treats the specific issues while keeping the people focused on a goal far greater than their own personal concerns or agendas.

To enjoy this unity, however, a continuing commitment to the specific doctrines of the Bible must be maintained. The day that a church exchanges the specific and unchanging teachings of God in the Bible for the relative opinions of men, is the day that the hold on the anchor of God's word loosens. The church will soon be adrift on a sea of relativism if her grip on the Bible is not firmly reset. Tossed by the crashing waves of political correctness, and battered by the winds of secularism, it will not be long before she and her witness sink and disappear completely from view.

Countless churches that once held firmly to the specific doctrines of the Bible lie broken and forgotten after willingly cutting themselves away from the anchor of God's word. The cutting often began with a call to reject the specific doctrines of the Bible, and they cut away one doctrine after another like the individual cords of a rope. One by one, doctrines that once defined what a church believed were no longer identifiable within the hearts and minds of the people. Churches turned to entertainment, political correctness, and acceptance from a world in open rebellion against God to fill the void created by the absence of deeply held belief, theological depth, and conviction of truth. The results are a nation in spiritual decline, lost amid relativism where the very idea that truth even exists is denied.

The spiritual picture in our nation is bleak, but it is not without hope. It may be that God will allow us to repent and reassert our hold on the anchor of the Bible. With this hope and prayer in mind, we will examine six specific doctrines in the following chapters that have defined what Christianity has believed about the Bible throughout history. They are not the only doctrines about the Bible, but they are essential doctrines, and to deny one of them is to deny or diminish each of the others. It is no wonder that Satan has attacked these six doctrines so relentlessly. His desire is to separate people from the truth of God's word. If he can cause a man to deny one or more of these six beliefs about the Bible, his work of deception will be much easier. Our nation has essentially denied all six of these truths, and as a result, Satan's work to confuse, deceive, and destroy her has never been easier. It is time for the church to fight back with the only weapon we have, the sword of the Spirit, which is the word of God. *(Eph. 6.7)*. Let us look more closely now at this sword and ensure we are familiar with its shape, weight, sharpness, and use.

Chapter 8 - The Authorship of Scripture

"But know this first of all, that no prophecy of Scripture is a matter of one's own interpretation, for no prophecy was ever made by an act of human will, but men moved by the Holy Spirit spoke from God." 2 Peter 1:20–21

The Bible states that all Scripture is inspired by God (*2 Tim. 3.16*). The Bible then is a book whose author is God Himself. In one sense, this is the sum of all that will be said in this chapter. Though it is a straightforward claim, God's authorship of the Bible does not always carry the weight in our lives that it should. This is especially true for those who were taught this fundamental tenet of

Christianity from childhood. Most children taken to church from the time they are infants grow up believing that God is the author of Scripture. I do not remember the first time I was taught that God was the author of the Bible, I grew up believing it because the people I loved and trusted told me it was true. I suspect this is the case for most Christians. However, many never undertake a deeper consideration of this simple, but foundationally important statement. Confronted with the doubt and skepticism of our age, many people at some point abandon the belief that God wrote the Bible. In the same way that it is difficult to know when they first started to believe as children, many people cannot tell you precisely when they stopped believing as adults. This is a common strategy used by Satan. He will at times exploit moments of crisis in our lives to cause us to turn from truth, but his more frequent method is to encourage a lifestyle that allows the truth to slip away gradually. People are often so busy living their lives they do not notice they are adrift with the world, and no longer attached to God by the anchor of His word.

To open the Bible is to open a book whose author is the King of kings and the Lord of lords. To read the Bible is to hear from the One who created each of us for His glory. To gain understanding of Scripture is to comprehend the thoughts of a mind so far greater than our own that comparison is simply not possible. Studying the Bible is to study the thoughts that God has deemed worthy of our knowing. These ideas should cause us to stop and thank God for the gift of His word. There should never be a time that we open the Bible casually without an acknowledgment and prayer of thanksgiving to God for His word. When the preacher opens the Bible to read his sermon text, the listener should lean in to hear what God has said. They should pray for the Spirit to enlighten their hearts and minds to the truth that God wants them to know. The daily reading and consideration of God's word is the path to blessing in our lives, and the hymn book of the Bible opens with this truth. Psalms chapter one tells us that the way of the blessed man is a way that includes meditation on the law of God *day and night. (Ps. 1.1-2).* I recall in my college years wondering just how far my spiritual life in Christ might advance if I studied my Bible at least as much as I studied my textbooks. We should not neglect our earthly studies, but surely, we ought to give at least equal weight to the hiding of God's word in our hearts as we do to the placing of the world's facts in our minds.

The sheer gravity of what it means that we have a book God wrote and addressed to us should stir us inwardly when we hold our bibles. There should be a catching of our spiritual breath as we read it, knowing that we are engaged in the reading of words that God has written. If we can open our Bibles and be unmoved, there must surely be something wrong inside us, and we ought to pray that God would help us understand why we are so cold and indifferent to His word. There is sure to be some sin, some doubt, fear, or selfishness that is preventing us from reading God's word correctly.

The Bible's Claim to Divine Authorship

If Christianity claims that God is the author of the Bible, then it must follow that the Bible makes this claim for itself. The entire Christian message falls apart if the Bible is nothing more than a collection of the writings of men, but the Bible clearly makes the claim for Divine authorship. It makes it plainly and repeatedly. It is not possible to read the Bible with an honest mind and come away without the knowledge that the Bible explicitly attests that it is the very word of God.

In chapter four I addressed the accusation that Christians use circular reasoning when arguing for the Bible's position as the source of absolute truth in the world. I provide here an additional defense against this accusation in the context of the Bible's claim that God is its author.

A correct and common answer to the question of why Christians believe the Bible is God's word is because the Bible says that it is God's word. The skeptic hears the circular argument and is quick to dismiss the Christian's claim without thinking more deeply about the issue and unfairness of their accusation. They dismiss the Christian message without a proper trial because they refuse to consider what the Bible itself says. But surely the Bible should be allowed a voice in any trial to determine the veracity of its own claims. Human courts allow the accused to speak on their own behalf, but the Bible is often never even read by those rejecting the claims it makes. In human courts, eyewitnesses are often counted on to help establish the truth. In the same way, the Bible ought to be given a chance to speak in the examination of the evidence that the Bible is the word of God. Further, the men who penned the Scripture are first-hand witnesses and should be allowed to give testimony as well. It would be a silencing of the accused and the key eyewitnesses to forbid the use of the Bible to validate its own claims to be God's word.

A lawyer who knows that a witness has damaging and convincing evidence against his client will do all he can to ensure that the witness never testifies in court. Should the efforts to prevent the witness from testifying prove unsuccessful, the lawyer will then do all he can to discredit and dismiss the witness and his testimony. It is plain to see that the enemy has been extraordinarily successful with this approach. He denies the claim that God is the author of the Bible and discredits anyone who makes the assertion. The Bible is then regarded as untrustworthy in the minds of many. It has been removed almost entirely from the arena of public debate and most dismiss the Bible having never read it themselves. They convict the Bible of being untrue without ever allowing the Bible the opportunity to speak for itself. A pillar of American law allows the accused to face his accusers. He has the right to give voice to his own defense. Why then, in the trial to determine the Bible's divine authorship, is the Bible so often not allowed to come to its own defense? Could it be because the enemy attorney in this trial knows that his case will suffer a devastating blow if he allows this witness to speak? The sections that follow represent key components of the Bible's defense regarding its claim of divine authorship.

∞

God's Authorship of The Old Testament

The first speaker in the Bible is God *(Gen. 1.3)*. The first words that carried across creation were words spoken by God. So, from the opening pages of the Old Testament we are told that we are reading the words of God. As we continue reading, we discover that God is the speaker in the Old Testament 13,574 times in 5,891 verses. God is being spoken to by man 3,473 times in 1,805 verses. One out of every three verses in the Old Testament contains words exchanged between God and man. Further, God speaks over three times for every one time that man speaks. If this were not enough, even the words spoken by man were often words that God had first given to him. God told Jeremiah that He had "...*put His words in his mouth...*" *(Jer. 1.9)*. God did the same for Moses *(Exo. 4.12)*, Ezekiel *(Eze. 13.1)*, Isaiah *(Isa. 49.1-2)*, Zechariah *(Zech. 4.8)* and others.

It is important to note that the claim to be a speaker for God was not made lightly. The punishment for falsely claiming to speak for God was severe and God called out any person who claimed to speak for Him who had not been called to do so. He condemns the false prophet and outlines severe punishment for the crime of claiming to speak for Him when they were speaking only for themselves. We find a key passage demonstrating this in

The Lost Anchor

Ezekiel chapter thirteen.

¹ And the word of the Lord came unto me, saying, ² Son of man, prophesy against the prophets of Israel that prophesy, and say thou unto them that prophesy out of their own hearts, Hear ye the word of the Lord; ³ Thus saith the Lord God; Woe unto the foolish prophets, that follow their own spirit, and have seen nothing! ⁴ O Israel, thy prophets are like the foxes in the deserts. ⁵ Ye have not gone up into the gaps, neither made up the hedge for the house of Israel to stand in the battle in the day of the Lord. ⁶ They have seen vanity and lying divination, saying, The Lord saith. and the Lord hath not sent them. and they have made others to hope that they would confirm the word. ⁷ Have ye not seen a vain vision, and have ye not spoken a lying divination, whereas ye say, The Lord saith it; albeit I have not spoken? ⁸ Therefore thus saith the Lord God; Because ye have spoken vanity, and seen lies, therefore, behold, I am against you, saith the Lord God. ⁹ And mine hand shall be upon the prophets that see vanity, and that divine lies. they shall not be in the assembly of my people, neither shall they be written in the writing of the house of Israel, neither shall they enter into the land of Israel; and ye shall know that I am the Lord God. (Eze. 13.1-9)

These verses serve as a warning to anyone who claims to speak on behalf of God. The preacher risks God's displeasure if he misrepresents what God has said. The man who enters the ministry without a call from God walks a dangerous path for himself, as well as for those to whom he ministers.

We see then that we are reading the words of God when we read the Old Testament. From God's direct speech, to His conversations with man and His warning to those who would falsely claim to speak for Him, seeing the Old Testament as something other than God's word is to miss what is in plain sight. Christians have not invented this claim. They have simply read the books of the Old Testament and concluded that the Bible is the word of God. The New Testament supports this conclusion when it states the Old Testament was given by inspiration of God *(2 Pet. 1.21)* and cites the Old Testament over two hundred times. Jesus Himself directly quoted from the Old Testament 28 times during His earthly ministry. The writers and speakers in the New Testament testify plainly that the scriptures of the Old Testament are God's words.

God's Authorship of the New Testament

Turning the page from the Old Testament to the New Testament does not change this picture. Nearly one third of the New Testament contains words spoken directly by Jesus, the Father, or the Holy Spirit. Four of the twenty-seven books focus entirely on the life of Christ and His teaching. The remaining books show what the followers of Christ did, said, and taught under the direction of the Holy Spirit. The Great Commission Christ left His people was to go and teach others what He had taught them *(Mat. 28.19-20)* and so it follows that what the disciples said, wrote, and taught in the New Testament was what Jesus Himself had instructed them to say, write, and teach. The book of Acts recounts the first thirty years of their efforts to obey the Lord's command. The remaining books of the New Testament, with the sole exception of Revelation, were written during those same thirty years. Each of these books contains words that Jesus and the Holy Spirit first spoke to His followers. The final book, Revelation, contains the words of God in prophecy, foretelling what will occur at the end of the world. With every turn of the page, the reader of the New Testament encounters the words of God. Like the Old Testament, Christians did not manufacture the idea that the New Testament contains the word of God. They do not make this claim to manipulate, intimidate, or appear superior. They make the claim because there is no other logical conclusion that can be reached. The Bible unquestionably claims to be the word of God. It is a dismissal of the entire message of the Bible to believe it to be anything less than what it claims to be.

Yet many people look at the Bible in just that light. A book written by men and not God. The results have not been good for the church, the Christian, or the world. If a man does not live by bread alone but by the word of God, a fact that both the Old and New Testaments affirm (Dt. 8.3, Mat. 4.4), then we are living in a starving world. Far too many churches are trying to keep people entertained so they do not notice their spiritual starvation. They design the church service to take people's minds off their hunger with a good song or a sermon that tells them they are okay. Or perhaps a message that provides only moral clichés and practical advice about how to get along in the world. Everything is carefully prepared except the food they truly need, the word of God. The dining room is beautiful, and the dishes are the best money can buy. The lighting is perfect and the music soothing. The table is meticulously set. The servants in their white gloves are standing at the ready to serve life sustaining nourishment. Thousands have gathered for the dinner. Promise after promise that the food will soon be ready is made, but it never appears. Week after week, the gathered crowd is encouraged to marvel at some new beauty in the room and the smartly dressed attendants. One can almost smell the food through sheer longing or wishful thinking. But the smell of food without the provision of food only makes matters worse. There are so many people nearby, and the empty promise of food has gone on for so long that a certain normalcy settles over the entire scene. The great danger in normalcy is that it can lead to complacency, and when that which is normal in our lives is dysfunctional, then we typically end up in dysfunctional complacency. We give up on finding peace with God, and the meaning and purpose which He intends for us to possess. The Bible is considered guilty by association in the view of many because they have been listening to people who claim to know its truth, but who have never partaken of its fruit themselves, and are in truth just as hungry as everyone else in the crowd. When someone at last gets hungry enough, however, no mere entertainment or dreaming will do. The beauty of the room fades. The entertainment grows wearisome and the sermon hollow with the lack of true spiritual nourishment. In these moments, a man would trade all the empty finery for a simple meal of true spiritual food. It is heartbreaking to think of the countless numbers of people who sit in church pews across our country who leave just as spiritually famished as they were when they arrived. There is a vast mission field today in the pews of Americanized Christianity which has substituted empty forms for the substance of the words of God in the Bible. This development has resulted largely because many no longer believe that God is the author of Scripture. The tragedy of this circumstance is compounded when we realize the Bible is indeed the word of God, and so the hunger is needless and avoidable.

Chapter 9 - The Authority of Scripture

"You shall therefore love the LORD your God, and always keep His charge, His statutes, His ordinances, and His commandments." Deuteronomy 11:1

Biblical Christianity maintains that the word of God is to have the final say in our churches, homes, and individual lives. This doctrine is referred to as the *Authority of Scripture*. It teaches that the Bible is to be the final arbiter in all disputes and ought to be the final guide in all decisions. Christians are not to appeal to their own opinions, feelings, or preferences as the final deciding factor in their choices. Nor are they to consider the words of others as ultimately authoritative. The Bible alone is to hold this position in the life of the child of God.

Adherence to the authority of the Bible has been a distinguishing mark of Christianity throughout history. Many consider that Martin Luther was single-handedly responsible for restoring this view to the church, but as instrumental as Luther's life and work were, there were protesters against the usurpation of Biblical authority long before he arrived on the scene in the 16th Century. These protesters spoke openly against the steady erosion of Biblical authority which had taken shape within much of Christianity over the many centuries since the Apostles. To say it another way, there were protesters long before the Protestant Reformation. In his book, Baptist Confessions of Faith, William Lumpkin writes,

"At the beginning of the sixteenth century there were people in every country of Western Europe who earnestly protested against corruption in the Church and who, therefore, welcomed the protests of Martin Luther and Ulrich Zwingli. Such were the people who came to be called Anabaptists. Having much in common with the churchly reformers, these folk at first were identified with their movements, and they separated from them only when the Reformation seemed to fall short of a full application of principles clearly enunciated by the Reformers.[7]".

---

[7]Lumpkin, William (1969). Baptist Confessions of Faith Revised Edition (p.11). Judson Press

Lumpkin also writes of the Lollards of the fourteenth century with whom John Wycliff was associated. Quoting Lumpkin again, he states "*The Lollards prepared no formal creeds or confessions of faith, their emphasis being rather upon the authority of the Scriptures...*[8]". Like the Lollards, other groups were hesitant to prepare confessions of faith for fear that their own confessions would eventually be granted the same authority as the Scripture. Their hesitation to prepare formal creeds based upon this fear bears clear testimony to their adherence to the authority of the Bible. When the word of man is given the same level of authority as the Bible, be that man a preacher, pastor, or priest, historical Christianity and the authoritative claims of the Bible have been abandoned.

As time passed, however, the danger of not specifically defining the beliefs held about God and His word were deemed more serious than the danger of replacing Scriptural authority by their introduction. Confessions of faith then began to explode onto the scene beginning in the sixteenth century, due in part to the invention of the printing press and the success of the reformers. In each of these confessions, a fundamental separating principle was the place of God's word as the supreme authority in the believer's life, and in the life and practice of the church. Many confessions could be cited that articulate that the Bible is the supreme standard

---

[8]Lumpkin, William (1969). Baptist Confessions of Faith Revised Edition (p.12). Judson Press

of the Christian faith. The one adopted by the author's church is provided here by way of example.

The New Hampshire Confession of Faith of 1853 on the Scriptures

"We believe that the Holy Bible was written by men divinely inspired, and is a perfect treasure of heavenly instruction (1); that it has God for its author, salvation for its end (2), and truth without any mixture of error for its matter (3); that it reveals the principles by which God will judge us (4); and therefore is, and shall remain to the end of the world, the true center of Christian union (5), and the supreme standard by which all human conduct, creeds, and opinions should be tried (6)".[9]

The final phrase in this statement makes the clear point that the Bible is the supreme standard of faith. No other source is to hold a higher authority than the Bible in the faith and practice of Christian people.

Stating this belief is much easier than *living* this belief, but it is the living of this belief that gives the words their weight and power. It has been said the actions of a man speak so loudly that what he says cannot be heard. I would encourage you to take a moment and read over the article of faith given above once again,

---

[9]Pendleton, J.M. (1966). Baptist Church Manual Revised (p.43-44). Broadman Press

and then consider your church, your home, and your own life. Does the Bible hold this level of authority over your life? Or are your own opinions, traditions, comfort zones, and plans sitting in a higher place of authority than God's word?

The Christian is called to obey the word of God, whether doing so creates an easy path forward or a difficult one. Following God and obeying His word will often be considered impractical, difficult, and even unnecessary according to the wisdom of men. Pragmatism has long been a sharp weapon in Satan's warfare against the Bible. The commands in Scripture which are difficult to obey and call us to a life of sacrifice and obedience to God are dismissed as being infeasible in our modern world. The problem with this thinking is that God is not concerned primarily with what is practical -- He is concerned instead with what is right. Yet in far too many Christian circles, the false god of pragmatism holds court and decides far too many cases.

The only thing for the Christian to do once they understand what God has said in the Bible is to believe and obey what God has said. Wayne Grudem states the following in his Systematic Theology. *"The authority of Scripture means that all the words in Scripture are God's words in such a way that to disbelieve or disobey any word of Scripture is to disbelieve or disobey God*[10].*"*

The Bible is not a set of moral platitudes that we merely keep in mind as we go about doing what we want to do in our lives. Rather, it is the book by which our lives are to be led. Many consider the Christian life complex when it is instead a life of great clarity and simplicity. We are to read God's word, hide it in our hearts, and obey what it says. We do this because we know we are obeying God, not just empty and lifeless words on a page.

This is not to say that the Christian life is easy. There is a difference between *simple* and *easy*. Something can be simple and difficult at the same time. Running a mile in four minutes is not complicated. It is rather simple. Just run four laps on a track and run each lap in sixty seconds or less. The accomplishment of this feat, however, is extremely difficult. It requires great effort, discipline, and training. In like fashion, Christianity is not complicated, but it can be difficult. G.K. Chesterton once wrote, *"The Christian ideal has not been tried and found wanting, it has been found difficult, and left untried."*[11]. Jesus Himself distills the Christian life down to a single, two-part command, *"Love God and love man." (Mat. 22.37)*. That is not a complicated command. It is

---

[10]Grudem, W.A. (2004). Systematic Theology: an Introduction to Biblical Doctrine (p.73). Leicester, Englad; Grand Rapids, MI: Inter-Varsity Press; Zondervan Pub. House

[11]Chesterton, G.K. (2015). What's Wrong With the World (p.35). Open Road Media

simple to understand. So simple in fact that a child can understand it. Yet obeying this command is difficult while we live in a world that hates God and while we wrestle with our own carnal hearts and minds. It will require from the Christian great effort, discipline, and training *(1 Tim. 4.7)*.

There will be times when obedience to God's word will require every ounce of our strength. Circumstances will arise when doing what God has called us to in the Bible will be the most difficult thing we will ever do. Alongside the difficult path of obedience will lie the comfortable path of disobedience. The path of disobedience will cry out to our fallen nature and convince us of just how much better things would be on that path, but the siren song that lured us onto the path of disobedience, which sounded so comforting in the beginning, soon changes and we hear only an unpleasant chord that strikes fear into our hearts. What appeared to be a well-lit path quickly turns dark with the absence of the light of God's word. We are frequently surrounded by many others on the path of disobedience and often find momentary comfort by their presence. But deep within we know there is an absence of the One who matters most. Not far down the path of disobedience we stumble and then find ourselves alone and afraid in the darkness. When we reach the fork in the road where the path of obedience and disobedience diverge, we must hold to the conviction that the Bible is the word of God and holds authority over our lives. This conviction, this certainty and confidence in the Bible will be what sends you down the path of obedience in your life. It will be submission to the Bible's authority that will keep you on that path regardless of the difficulties you meet along the way.

∞

The Nature of the Authority of Scripture

The essential matter at hand in any discussion on the Authority of Scripture is obedience to God in the Persons of the Father, Son, and Holy Spirit. This is important because people often see the Bible as separate from the Persons of God. This error most often manifests itself in one of two extremes. The first extreme is a form of hyper spiritualism separated from the written word of God. The second is the attempt to live in obedience to the Bible but separated from the transforming power of a real and experiential knowledge of God through the regenerating work of the Holy Spirit. We should avoid both extremes at all costs, but sadly, I believe much of Christianity in America is now standing in one of these two extremes. Satan does not care which extreme you choose. He just wants to ensure you choose one of them. Our individual personalities and the collective personalities of churches will lean toward one of these extremes or the other and pastors should be on constant watch for either of them gaining a foothold in the church. We should also examine our own hearts to ensure one or the other is not setting up as the default position that guides our own view of the Bible and the Christian life. Under the guise of theology, Satan presents a false choice where men must choose between submission to the Spirit of God, or submission to the word of God. Yet, as we have seen, it was God Himself who wrote the Bible. We cannot separate the author of a book from the book itself. How one thinks of the Bible is how one will eventually think of the God of the Bible. How one thinks of the God of the Bible is how one will eventually think of the Bible.

The false choice that Satan presents has the power to cripple the Christian faith. For this reason, we should understand that the authority of the Scripture assumes the working of both the word, and the Spirit. For the Christian faith to be real in our lives, the Spirit and the word must both be active participants. I have witnessed both false extremes in my life, and I have seen firsthand the havoc that Satan has made of the church as well as people's lives in either case.

The first extreme is the position that the Spirit of God works apart from His word. In these settings, feelings, emotions, and personal opinions often usurp the position of authority which the word of God alone ought to have. What a person feels becomes more important than what the word of God states. Encouragements to follow one's own feelings are heard more often than encouragement to follow the word of God. Over time, what a person feels in their heart becomes the true authority. With the best of intentions, men become followers of the feelings of fallen creatures rather than the word of a righteous and holy God. So long as words like, "*I feel*", or "*I believe in my heart*" begin a sentence, many ideas contrary to the Bible take root in the church. It is as though there is no recognition that God has warned us that "*The heart is deceitful above all things, and desperately wicked; who can know it?*" *(Jer. 17.9)*. No honest person can deny that their hearts have imagined things so vile they would run away in shame should others come to know those thoughts. Our carnal hearts are untrustworthy things, and even when the heart of a man is right before God, the *rightness* of his heart is measured by his heart's alignment with God's word.

This extreme is highly susceptible to religious manipulation. Music is often used to stir emotions and people then regard those emotions as manifestations of the working of the Spirit. A preacher uses stories to tug at the heart of his hearers or someone testifies with great emotion and sincerity about their problems or struggles. In these cases, the response is often a human response to a human message. It is not a response driven by the conviction of the Holy Spirit over sin or the Lordship of Jesus Christ.

A red flag that this extreme has set up in the heart or within the church is that commitments to God are short-lived. Revivals last days or perhaps weeks, but then life continues much as it was before. There is no real and lasting change that takes place. The fire might have burned brightly, but it burned for only a short time. These fires burn only briefly because the emotions that fuel them quickly burn out and people can then become revival surfers or preacher stalkers. Like an addict they jump from church to church, preacher to preacher, revival to revival seeking their next spiritual high as they look for something to fuel the emptiness they feel in their lives. However, the high never lasts and they find themselves empty once again. The normalcy bias slips in and people think this is the best the Christian life has to offer. A hope that, from time to time at least, during the annual revival perhaps, or when a visiting preacher comes, God will come on the scene and the spiritual high will return, but this is not the life of deep, lasting, and constant joy that God desires for His people.

A second red flag is the inconsistency of the Christian life that follows this extreme. Rather than a settled and mature child of God who is content with God in all circumstances, one holding to this extreme is tossed violently by the circumstances of life. Emotions are a two-edged sword. The spiritual highs that are experienced are balanced by the spiritual lows that always follow. My sincere prayer is that God would open our eyes to this extreme and help us realize He has given us His word to live by and enjoy every day. His word is a fountain that never runs dry. His word ought to be the delight of our lives and the subject of our ongoing meditation and consideration. His word brings us to Him, which is the entire point of life itself, much less the Christian walk. When we are with God in His word daily, we discover joy, peace and blessing regardless of the specific circumstances of our lives. We no longer seek only the spiritual mountaintops, but we seek to walk through the valley with God as well. Our lives are defined by a consistent spiritual joy in God, not a sporadic roller coaster of religious emotion.

The damage done when a church believes that the Spirit of God works separately from His word explains in part the existence of the second extreme. A valid fear of the dangers of the first extreme leads to an overcorrection. In this second extreme, the working of the Holy Spirit in the mind and heart are considered unnecessary, or worse, unreal. The Scriptures are considered the *fullness* of God rather than the *expression* of God. Knowledge and mental consent are considered the pinnacle of Christian experience rather than relationship and obedience. The words of the Bible become separate from the Person who wrote the Bible, namely God. It is then said that knowing God is defined by having a mere knowledge of what God has written. So long as there is an intellectual agreement with the Bible, a person is proclaimed a Christian.

When Jesus confronted this extreme in Nicodemus, He spoke plainly about the requirement of the new birth to be saved (Jn. 3.3). Clearly then, knowledge of God's word apart from the working of the Spirit of God is not enough to reach heaven. Jesus makes this point again when He states that He will say *"Depart from me, I never knew you."* to those who claimed to be His followers but never truly came to know Him. *(Mat. 7.23)* Those who claim that one can be saved by the simple repeating of a prayer, or the repeating of a verse fall into this extreme. The Bible becomes something akin to a mystical force where the words are thought to have a power of their own. But words communicate meaning. Words on their own apart from their meaning are powerless to accomplish their intended purpose. This is true for God's word as well as any other. Nowhere do we read in God's word that a mere repetition of the words of the Bible can save. If that were true, and the virtue were in the words themselves, would we not be required to repeat the verses of Scripture in their original Greek? As close as our English translations can come to the original, are not the English words still different from the

Greek? Is it not clear that becoming a Christian and following God involves the ongoing working of the Spirit of God in the heart to make the words real to us on a personal level? When Job cried out, *"I know my redeemer lives"*, was his certainty based on his knowledge that there were writings about a redeemer? Or did his certainty come because he *knew* his Redeemer? *(Job 19.25)* Does your faith stand in the power of God? Or does it stand in the wisdom of men? *(1 Cor. 2.5)* Do you truly know God? Or do you know only the writings about God?

This principle is taught in the Old Testament during Israel's forty-year wilderness wandering. In Numbers chapter twenty-one, God sends serpents among the people because of their unbelief and impatience. *(Num. 21.5-6)* Moses prays for the people and God tells Moses to make a bronze serpent. Moses is then to let Israel know that if anyone was struck by a serpent, they were to look to the bronze serpent. If they looked, their life would be spared. If they did not look, they would die. The picture being painted is a picture of salvation. What the people looked to when they looked upon the bronze serpent was the grace and mercy of God for their sin. Yet, hundreds of years later during the reign of king Hezekiah in Judah, the bronze serpent had become an idol. *(2 Ki. 18.4)* That which was meant to *symbolize* God and *communicate His message* to God's people was thought to have virtue apart from the power of God. Hezekiah's response to this misplaced confidence was to identify the bronze serpent as merely a piece of brass and he broke it in pieces. This was done to remind the people that mercy, grace, and power have always been in God Himself, not the things God might use at certain times to communicate His message. In many places the Bible has become like the bronze serpent -- valued highly but misunderstood to be the instrument God has designed to bring people into an *actual* relationship with Him.

∞

The history of Christianity is littered with many examples where an over correction against one extreme led to an error in the other extreme. God does not work apart from His word. The word of God should rule over our feelings and emotions. Yet, our understanding of the word of God should bring joy to the heart, and deep satisfaction, peace, purpose, and meaning to our lives as we enjoy fellowship with God. The entire person, our emotions and our thoughts should be brought into subjection to God's word. The answer is not to dismiss emotion in favor of the intellect, or the intellect in favor of emotion.

Edgar Young Mullins summarizes these thoughts well in his book, "*The Christian Religion in its Doctrinal Expression*". There Mullins writes,

"...the Bible remains in its place of authority for Christians. It is a vital and living authority, and not a mechanical and ecclesiastical one. It is our authoritative source of information as to the historical revelation of God in Christ. It is regulative of Christian experience and Christian doctrine. It is the instrument of the Holy Spirit in his regenerative and sanctifying influences. As

regulative and authoritative it saves us from subjectivism on the one hand and from a bare rationalism on the other. It holds us to the great saving deeds of God in Jesus Christ, the Redeemer and Lord. It is final for us in all the matters of our Christian faith and practice[12]."

Christianity is not a life led by spiritual subjectivity. Nor is it a life led by what Mullins called a `bare rationalism". Submitting to the Authority of Scripture involves the submission of both our minds and our hearts to the *word* and *Person* of God. Recovering the lost anchor of the Bible then must include a recovery of the authority it is to have over our lives.

---

[12] Mullins, E. Y. (1917). The Christian Religion in Its Doctrinal Expression (p. 153). Philadelphia; Boston; St. Louis; Los Angeles; Chicago; New York; Toronto: Roger Williams Press.

Chapter 10 - The Selection of Scripture

"The word which came to Jeremiah from the LORD, saying, "Thus says the LORD, the God of Israel, 'Write all the words which I have spoken to you in a book." Jeremiah 30:1–2

A common question regarding the Bible is whether all sixty-six books that are included in the Bible should have been. A related question is whether there are books that were not included that should have. These questions have to do with a concept known as the *Canon of Scripture*. The Canon of Scripture is a term used to identify the books of divine authorship and therefore worthy to be included in the Bible. The central issue is whether the Bible includes all the books that it should include and none of the books that it should not. The weight of the claims made regarding the Authorship and Authority of Scripture means that the Canon of Scripture is an important topic for our consideration. After all, if the Christian is to commit his life in obedience to God through His word, confirming that the Bible includes *only* the right books, and *all* the right books, is essential. This is the issue that will be examined in this chapter.

It is important to note that the Bible I am referring to is the Bible known as the *Protestant Bible*. While I am not overly fond of this title (I believe the Canon precedes the Protestant Reformation) it is the most direct way to distinguish between the Canon of Scripture as identified by the Catholic denomination, and the Bible used by non-Catholic denominations. The primary difference between the Catholic and non-Catholic Bible is the inclusion of the books known as the *Apocrypha* in the Catholic Bible. More will be said of the Apocrypha later, but for now, the point to keep in mind is that the Protestant Bible is in view in this chapter.

I will provide only a summary of the primary issues at hand regarding the Canon of Scripture. Others have written on this subject in much greater detail. The brevity on this subject should not be interpreted as a sign that the Canon of Scripture is uncertain. On the contrary, Christians can have great confidence that the Bible they read contains all the books that it should contain, and none of the books that it should not. I recommend to the reader who desires a deeper study of the canon of Scripture "*A General Introduction to the Bible, Revised and Expanded*" by Norman Geisler and William Nix. Wayne Grudem's *Systematic Theology* also treats the canon of Scripture with great clarity and depth.

∞

The Old Testament Canon

God gave specific calls to men to write His words throughout the Old Testament. He told Moses to write the Law He had given him in a book and store it in the Ark of the Covenant. *(Deut. 31.24-26)* God said that the king in Israel was to

"write him a copy of this law in a book out of that which is before the priests the Levites. And it shall be with him, and he shall read there all the days of his life. that he may learn to fear the Lord his God, to keep all the words of this law and these statutes, to do them." (Deut. 17.18-19).

God told Jeremiah to write in a book all the words He had spoken to him. *(Jer. 30.2)* God gave Isaiah a similar command when He told him to write what He had said in a book so that the book would be a witness against his rebellious and lying children *(Isa. 30.8-9)*. The phrase, *"saith the LORD "* appears 841 times in 802 verses in the Old Testament. From Genesis to Malachi, the thirty-nine books of the Old Testament bear witness that they are books penned by men but authored by God. As a result, the clear testimony of the books themselves regarding their divine authorship bears witness to their rightful place in the Bible.

God called various men to write His words throughout Israel's history and Israel carefully gathered and collected those writings and each time they recognized a book to be from God, they added it to the Canon of Scripture. This is a highly simplified definition of the process of canonization, but it captures the essence of what was done. The exact process used to determine a book's worthiness to be included in the Old Testament canon is unknown, but the results of the process speak clearly for its legitimacy. The thirty-nine books of the Old Testament have been accepted by most scholars - scholars who have spent countless hours researching this issue. The fact that there have been no serious or lasting objections to the list of the books of the Old Testament provides us with great confidence that the list is accurate.

Another significant witness to the validity of the canon of the Old Testament is the clear break between the Old Testament and the New Testament. No books were recognized as Scripture after the 430's B.C. with the completion of Malachi until the opening of the New Testament over 400 years later. There were many other writings during this time, but none of them were considered Scripture. The Jewish historian Josephus gives us insight into Israel's view that no new prophecies had come after Malachi when he states,

"It is true, our history hath been written since Artaxerxes very

particularly, but hath not been esteemed of the like authority with the former by our forefathers, because there hath not been an exact succession of prophets since that time;[13]"

Josephus explained that while various histories of the Jewish people had been written that covered the time between Artaxerxes and Josephus' own day, none of those writings were considered Scripture. From this we learn that there were unique and identifiable markers in the writings of the books that were Canonized and placed in Scripture, and those that owed their existence to mere human authorship. Josephus is not the only one who expressed this sentiment, but his position as a respected historian reveals the prevalence of the belief in Israel that no new prophecies had come from God since the days of Malachi. So, in the view of Israel, the Old Testament revelation came to an end at that time.

If the process used to select the books of the Old Testament had not been carefully considered, surely, we would have more than thirty-nine books. There also would surely have been books that made the list written after Malachi. The clear stopping point of the Old Testament provides an important clue into how the Canon was established. The Jews regarded their role in the

---

[13]Josephus, F., & Whiston, W. (1987). The works of Josephus: complete and unabridged (p. 776). Peabody: Hendrickson.

canonization process as one of *identification* and not *selection*. In other words, they looked for divine markers that revealed that a book was worthy of being included in the Canon of Scripture. They were not selecting the books so much as they were identifying them. Their identification processes no doubt considered the writer and his standing as a prophet of God and there were certainly other identifying markers as well. Though we do not have an authoritative list of what those identifying marks were, we do have the list of books that were identified using them. This allows for the ability to reverse engineer at least some of what those identifiers must have been. The list of books included in the Old Testament has proven to be nearly universally accepted for over 2,000 years, and the proof of the validity of the process is bolstered by the longevity of the results of the process.

What about the concern that there are books that should be in the Old Testament but are not? Are there "*lost books*" of the Bible that have somehow been overlooked? Occasionally Hollywood or a modern-day false prophet will create quite a stir about the possibility that there are other inspired books that are not included in the Bible. It is ultimately impossible to prove a negative, and this is all the cover Hollywood, or the religious charlatan needs to make money on "*what if*" scenarios. However, if there are lost books, then we would not know about them since they would be *lost* books. To speculate on unknown things is the height of sophistry and is often nothing more than an attempt to distract from what is clear and known. Still, the question of whether there are lost books can be answered in the negative with great confidence. Nowhere in the New Testament do we read that Jesus, or the Apostles, disagreed with the Jews in the books that made up the Old Testament. The Canon of the Old Testament was settled hundreds of years before Christ. The Greek translation of the Old Testament (the Septuagint) was known and read by many. The absence of a dispute in the New Testament over the makeup of the Old Testament gives clear testimony that there was no credible disagreement over the books that should have been included in the Old Testament. Jesus did not say that the Jews were misguided because they were not reading the *right* books or didn't have *all* the books they needed. He said they were misguided because they *misunderstood* the books they already had. The Jewish nation was not lost because they did not have the correct books -- they were lost because they denied the teachings found in the books already given, and the same is true for us today.

The New Testament Canon

Turning to the question of the canon of the New Testament, we find similar certainty that we have all the right books and none of the wrong ones. Twenty-two of the twenty-seven books of the New Testament were written by Apostles. The Apostles were eyewitnesses to Christ and were taught directly by Him. They were provided special training by Jesus Himself and thus had a unique authority in the early church to communicate the teachings of Christ to others. The remaining five books, Mark, Luke, Acts, Hebrews, and Jude, while not written by Apostles, bear clear marks of divine authorship. With the books of Mark, Luke, and Acts, Apostolic confirmation of these books is clearly implied since these books record events directly experienced by the Apostles who were still living when these books were written. Hebrews has proved to be the most contested book in the New Testament canon. Many assume Pauline authorship, which would put the question to rest, but the writer of Hebrews does not identify himself and there is considerable debate about whether Paul is in fact the author of the book. It is difficult to be dogmatic on the issue of authorship in Hebrews since the book itself does not answer the question. However, the sheer majesty of the book and consistency to other books convinced the early church to adopt it as Scripture. The great harmony that Hebrews brings between the Old Covenant and the New Covenant cannot be denied, and one can hardly imagine not recognizing the book of Hebrews as Scripture with its significant contribution to the full view of faith and its clear explanation of how the Old Testament ceremonial law pointed to Christ. With the book of Jude, his close connection with James and being a brother of Jesus carried much weight. By the end of the 4th Century A.D., the New Testament canon had been firmly and officially established, and the collection of books in the Bible was complete. As with the Old Testament, there have been no significant disagreements over the twenty-seven books of the New Testament, and surely there would have been if legitimate reasons existed for such disagreement.

∞

The Apocrypha

The books of the Apocrypha are the fourteen additional books that are included in the Catholic Bible that are not in the Protestant Bible. They were written during the 400 years between the Old and New Testaments. The precise number of apocryphal books is itself a matter of dispute. The Eastern Orthodox church does not recognize the same list as the Roman Catholic church. The Roman Catholic list is as follows.

- 1 Esdras
- 2 Esdras
- Tobit
- Judith
- Rest of Esther
- Wisdom
- Ecclesiasticus
- Baruch and the Epistle of Jeremy
- Song of the Three Children
- Story of Susanna
- The Idol Bel and the Dragon
- Prayer of Manasses
- 1 Maccabees
- 2 Maccabees

There is much that could be said of these books and this list itself. My intention here is not to provide an exhaustive description of how any of the various lists were collected. Rather, I aim to provide a few reasons why these books have not been considered canonical by nearly all non-Catholics.

∞

The books of the Apocrypha are never quoted in the New Testament. Jesus Himself never quotes from any of them in His teaching and preaching. This is significant because the version of the Old Testament from which Jesus and the New Testament writers most often quoted was the Greek translation of the Old Testament known as the Septuagint. The Septuagint included at least some of the apocryphal writings and so the lack of a single quotation in the New Testament appears to have been a deliberate choice by Jesus and the other writers of the New Testament. Perhaps one could argue that some New Testament passages *allude* to writings found in the apocryphal books, but at no point does a New Testament writer quote directly from the Apocrypha.

It is also interesting no note that while the Jews recognized the thirty-nine books of the Old Testament hundreds of years before Christ, the Apocrypha was not officially accepted as Scripture until the Roman Catholic Council of Trent (A.D. 1545-1563) nearly 2,000 years after the canonicity of the other books had been clearly established. The timing of the acceptance of these books, many of which include support for ideas such as praying for the dead, and salvation by works, is suspicious given the ongoing doctrinal disputes in the 16th Century between Catholicism and what is now popularly called Protestantism.

∞

Commentaries among the people of the Jewish Qumran community (where the Dead Sea scrolls were discovered) do not address any apocryphal books even though they were found among their collections. It seems clear then that this important community did not consider the books of the Apocrypha as canonical. The different treatment of the books of the Apocrypha by the people of Qumran provides another clue that the apocryphal books were not viewed on the same level as the books of the accepted Old Testament canon by the Jewish people.

Finally, and most importantly, there are serious doctrinal errors and issues of accuracy in the apocryphal books. The Bible's message that salvation is not dependent on human effort is clear from Genesis to Revelation, but the Apocrypha contradicts this teaching. Tobit 4:11 states, "*For alms deliver from all sin, and from death, and will not suffer the soul to go into darkness.*" Tobit 12:9 states, "*For alms delivereth from death, and the same is that which purgeth away sins, and maketh to find mercy and life everlasting.*" The teaching that the giving of alms provides salvation has placed a lot of money in Catholic coffers, but I fear it has also placed many souls in eternal ruin.

In addition to the theological errors in the Apocrypha, there are also clear historical errors as well. The book of Judith claims that Nebuchadnezzar was the king of the Assyrians, not the Babylonians. The book of Baruch states that Israel would live in exile in Babylon for seven generations where the books of the Old Testament state, and the record of history shows, that the exile lasted seventy years. Many of the writings in the Apocrypha can only be described as fanciful and do not hold the weight of inspired text. Leveraging the process that was used to identify divinely written words, Jewish scholars identified the books of the Apocrypha as being of human origin, and thus they did not include them in the Canon of Scripture.

Confidence in God

While the evidence for the legitimacy of the process used in the canonization of the Bible is significant, we must recognize that there are still questions surrounding canonization that are difficult to answer with precision. As has been stated, we have lost the exact process the Jews used to identify the books of the Old Testament and are left with only the results of the process. The results speak quite clearly for themselves, but those who desire to cast doubt on the Scripture will focus on these areas of perceived ambiguity and weakness. There are still people today who, like the Pharisees of Jesus day, love to *"strain out a gnat and swallow a camel." (Mat. 23.24)*. Questions about Hebrews, Jude, and even the writings of Paul are sometimes called into question. There are many who have honest questions about the reliability of the canon of Scripture, and to all these questions, I would encourage a consideration of the evidence we have provided here, along with the evidence others have provided elsewhere. Yet I do not point to this evidence and these hard facts alone. I appeal to a trust of God to ensure His people have the books He intends for them to have, no more and no less. For the skeptic who reads this they will see weakness but for the believer in God there ought to be great confidence. God sent His Son to die on a cross and pay the penalty of sin for lost mankind. Would He not then ensure that the writings He has left us to tell us that story would include all the right books and none of the wrong ones? For my part, I trust fully that God took the necessary care to ensure that the Bible we read is the Bible He intends for us to read. The historical record affirms this trust, but it does not replace or supersede my trust in God's providential care over His word.

Chapter 11 - The Inerrancy of Scripture

"Every word of God is tested; He is a shield to those who take refuge in Him." Proverbs 30:5

The inerrancy of Scripture represents a key battle in the effort to maintain a hold on the anchor of the Bible. In a very real sense, to deny the inerrancy of Scripture is to deny the Bible itself. To disavow inerrancy is to turn away from an essential doctrine of Christianity. For these reasons and others, the doctrine of inerrancy faces a relentless assault from those who openly reject the Bible and Christianity, but this doctrine also faces opposition from the pulpits and pews of liberal Christianity. While the unbelieving world can tolerate *some* of the beliefs that Christians hold about the Bible, the inerrancy of Scripture is a doctrine that many simply refuse to accept. Belief in the inerrancy of the Bible cannot coexist with the present-day belief that absolute truth does not exist. The logic is that if absolute truth does not exist, then an inerrant Bible that claims to identify absolute truth cannot exist either.

In this chapter we will discover that the doctrine of inerrancy divides the secular and biblical worldviews as few other doctrines do. It is important to realize that belief in the inerrancy of Scripture is an "*either, or*" issue. Each of us must choose a side. There are those who maintain that one can be Christian yet deny the inerrancy of the Bible, but we will either stand with the Inerrancy of Scripture or we will end up standing against the Scripture. We cannot believe portions of the Bible that we deem believable and disregard the rest without making the assertion that the Bible is unworthy of our trust and obedience.

If the Bible is not inerrant, how is one to know which parts of the Bible are trustworthy, and which parts are not? If I know that a certain person is given to lying, how can I trust anything they say? I will be continually looking for confirming evidence that what that person tells me is in fact true. Their word alone will never be enough. This will be especially true if I am relying on this person for information that will have a significant impact on my life. In the same way, if I believe that parts of the Bible are wrong, how can I trust any of it? It might be argued that we can trust the parts of the Bible that we know are true via some other means of confirmation. We might say we can trust the Bible when it records the ascensions of the nations of Assyria, Babylon, Persia, and Rome, because history confirms that this is an accurate record. In this case, we are not placing our trust in the Bible but in recorded history. Once we make the assertion that the Bible is untrustworthy (either directly or indirectly), we assert that the God which the Bible speaks of is untrustworthy as well.

Denying the inerrancy of Scripture is a slippery slope that will end in the open denial of all the Bible says. The enemy knows this and it makes his job of deceiving the nations easier. He does not have to convince a person, initially, that the entire Bible is wrong. He need only convince them that a *certain portion* of the Bible is wrong. Once he has convinced them that one portion of the Bible is wrong, he will convince them that another portion is wrong. And then another, and another, and another. Soon, the entire Bible is thought to be full of errors and belief in the inerrancy of the Bible is abandoned altogether.

The Definition of Inerrancy

The first task in holding to the inerrancy of Scripture is to establish what is meant by the term *inerrancy*. Several definitions for inerrancy have been provided through the years by various theologians, but for our purposes, *the inerrancy of Scripture means that the Bible is a perfect record of true facts*. All that the Bible claims is true, is in fact, true. All that the Bible claims is untrue, is in fact, untrue. Borrowing a phrase from the New Hampshire Confession of Faith, the Bible contains *"truth without any mixture of error for its matter."* Stated simply, the inerrancy of Scripture means that the Bible contains no errors.

The Bible itself is the source from which the doctrine of Inerrancy is derived, as it was for the Authority and Authorship of Scripture. We find a foundational text on the inerrancy of Scripture in Paul's second letter to Timothy. In that letter Paul writes, *"All Scripture is given by inspiration of God, and is profitable for doctrine, for reproof, for correction, for instruction in righteousness." (2 Tim. 3.16)* The word Scripture in this passage is translated from the Greek word, *graphe*, which in the Bible refers specifically to the words God inspired men to write. God is Himself perfect (*Mat. 5.48*) and does not lie. *(Pro. 30.5)* When these complementing thoughts are placed together, the only conclusion that can be reached is that the words God had men write are perfect, true, and without error and there is no other rational conclusion that can be reached. If God is perfect and will not lie, then all He says must be true. Norman Geisler and William Nix, in their book, *A General Introduction to the Bible*, write, *"To deny the inerrancy of Scripture is to impugn either the integrity of God or the identity of the Bible as the Word of God.*[14]*"* If we believe what the Bible says about God, then we must also believe

---

[14]Geisler, N. L., & Nix, W. E. (1986). A General Introduction to the Bible (Rev. and expanded., p. 55). Chicago: Moody Press.

that the Bible is inerrant. To believe something other than this is to believe a contradiction.

∞

Rightly Applying Inerrancy. A Word on Bible Translation

It is important that we apply inerrancy correctly once we understand its meaning. Claiming that the sixty-six books of the Bible, penned by dozens of authors over fifteen centuries, is inerrant, is indeed a bold claim. So bold in fact that many people dismiss the claim immediately. They open the Bible and find what they believe is an error and they dismiss the claim of inerrancy, but many of the challenges to inerrancy center around how it is applied, rather than on the claims of the doctrine itself. The question we must ask is, "*What is specifically in view when we say that the Bible is inerrant?*"

The inerrancy of Scripture refers to the original writings of the Old and New Testaments. Inerrancy cannot be properly applied to any of the various translations of the Bible. When God spoke the words of Scripture to men, He inspired particular men, at particular times, to write in particular languages. Inerrancy then, can only be applied to the original Hebrew and Aramaic of the Old Testament and the Greek of the New Testament. To claim inerrancy for any translation, we must also claim that God inspired men in the translation of His word as well as in the original writing of His word, but this belief is unnecessary, dangerous, and contradictory. It is unnecessary because the Scripture itself does not support or even require the claim. It is dangerous because to apply inerrancy to any translation puts far too much authority in the hands of human translators. The original writers of the Bible were not translators, but agents through which God wrote. We see proof of this throughout much of the Dark Ages when the Bible was locked up in Latin, a language that the common person could not read. Without the ability to read God's word for themselves the people were reliant upon the Priests to tell them what God expected of them. The abuses this gave rise to are many and beyond the scope of this book. Suffice it to say that when God's words are filtered through men, care must always be taken that those men are truly speaking God's words, and not their own.

Believing that God inspired the translation of Scripture is contradictory because the Bible states that written revelation was completed with the book of Revelation. God gave warning that no one should add to or take away from what had been written. *(Rev. 22.18)* If that is true, it is contradictory to claim that God inspired men with new words to write after the completion of the book of Revelation. Even if the argument is made that they are the *same words* in a different language, it still stands that they are *new words*. Language is an art as well as a science, and translation involves the choosing of specific words to translate words from the original language into the new. For a translation of the Bible to be inerrant, it would have to be affirmed that God was the one specifically choosing the words in the new translation, but there is no claim by orthodox Christian translators that they were being given divine word choices in their work. Their task was to translate as closely as possible in the new language, what God had said in the original languages.

This is not to say one must learn the original languages of the Scripture to rightly understand the Bible. More will be said about this in a later chapter covering the *Clarity of Scripture*. The point here is that the translation of the Bible into different languages is not only proper, but it is a key activity in the fulfillment of the Great Commission. Jesus commanded His followers to teach all men what He had first taught them, and the translation of Scripture into other languages is a fundamental component in obeying this command of the Lord. I am grateful to God for prompting men and women to translate the Scripture and for providentially watching over the work of translation into the languages of the world. While sharing the Gospel in countries where the people did not speak English, I have been grateful that the people were holding Bibles written in their own languages. I am humbled by the sacrifices of John Wycliffe, William Tyndale, Adoniram Judson and his wife Ann, and countless others who dedicated their lives to the translation of the Scripture so that the common man could read God's word.

The translation of God's word represents the arming of an entire people group with the only offensive weapon a Christian possesses, and it ensures that if people desire to defend themselves against the lies of the enemy they can be properly armed for the task. It allows mothers and fathers to point their children to the truth of God's word to combat the deceptions they hear from the world. It provides for the preacher the entire set of doctrines he is to teach the believer and unbeliever alike in a language he and his hearers understand. It provides for every believer the ability to defend themselves against error, whether that error comes from outside the church or from their own pews and pulpits.

∞

It bears noting that Jesus and the Apostles themselves approved of the work of translation. The Hebrew Old Testament was translated into Greek in the Septuagint before Jesus came to the world, and an examination of the New Testament quotations of the Old Testament reveals that the wording used to quote the Old Testament was often the wording found in the Septuagint, not the original Hebrew. Jesus' use of the Septuagint wording is nothing less than a divine endorsement of the translation of Scripture. Unlike the faith of Islam, which forbids the translation of the Quran into any other language, God has explicitly approved the translation of the Bible. His implicit approval is also understood by His clear command to take His word to the entire world. In addition to this implicit approval, God provided His explicit approval of translation at Pentecost when people who spoke many different languages all heard the truth of the Gospel in their native tongue as recorded in Acts chapter two.

"And when the day of Pentecost was fully come, they were all with one accord in one place. And suddenly there came a sound from heaven as of a rushing mighty wind, and it filled all

the house where they were sitting. And there appeared unto them cloven tongues like as of fire, and it sat upon each of them. And they were all filled with the Holy Ghost, and began to speak with other tongues, as the Spirit gave them utterance. And there were dwelling at Jerusalem Jews, devout men, out of every nation under heaven. Now when this was noised abroad, the multitude came together, and were confounded, because that every man heard them speak in his own language. And they were all amazed and marvelled, saying one to another, Behold, are not all these which speak Galilaeans? And how hear we every man in our own tongue, wherein we were born? Parthians, and Medes, and Elamites, and the dwellers in Mesopotamia, and in Judaea, and Cappadocia, in Pontus, and Asia, Phrygia, and Pamphylia, in Egypt, and in the parts of Libya about Cyrene, and strangers of Rome, Jews and proselytes, Cretes and Arabians, we do hear them speak in our tongues the wonderful works of God." (Acts 2.1–11)

Though we should recognize the benefit and use of translations, we must understand that translations performed by men have not been directly inspired by God in the same way as the original writings. As a result, we must not apply inerrancy to a translation. When we are reading a translation of the Bible, we are reading words chosen by translators. This does not mean that translations are inherently untrustworthy, it simply means that we must not apply inerrancy to them. To do so would be to make a translator's words equal with God's words.

The Lost Anchor

∞

The choice of a translation is not in view in this book, but a few words of encouragement are provided here for how we might measure the relative trustworthiness of a specific translation.

A fundamental part of the translation process involves the determination of the translational approach that will be used. There is a great deal of nuance related to Bible translation but there are two primary approaches I want to cover. The first approach is generally called *Formal Equivalence*. A formal equivalent translation focuses on a *word-for-word* translation. Formal equivalent translations error on the side of accuracy in translating each word and are less concerned about the ease of readability. Examples of formal equivalent translations are the King James Version, American Standard Version, and English Standard Version. The second approach is known as *Dynamic (or Functional) Equivalence*. A dynamic equivalent approach is a *thought-for-thought* translation and the concern shifts from accurately translating each *word* to accurately translating each *thought*. This shift in focus is primarily an effort to aid in the readability of the Bible. Examples of Bibles that have been translated using the dynamic equivalent method are the New International Version, The Amplified Bible, and the New Living Translation. Measuring the relative trustworthiness of any translation is aided by understanding the method of translation that was used. A formal equivalent translation will be closer to the original languages than a dynamic equivalent translation, due simply to the fact that its intention is to translate each word as accurately as possible. A thought for thought approach can easily (and even unintentionally) cross the line from *translation* to *interpretation*. A Dynamic Equivalent translation risks providing for the reader the thought the translator believes is in the text and can misdirect them from God's intended meaning in the text. This should give us pause when reading these translations as there is a higher risk of moving further away from the inerrant word of God in the original languages. This does not mean dynamic equivalent translations are without value, but it does mean that we should not base our understanding of the word of God on these translations alone.

The Necessity and Work of the Spirit

The inability to attribute inerrancy to translations is unsettling for some Christians and it can create a concern about whether the Bible we read is reliable. Some have met this concern by suggesting that a particular translation has been divinely approved to the exclusion of all others. This is an unfortunate and unnecessary response. It is unfortunate because it has often caused division between Christian people, and it is unnecessary because it displaces where the Christian's trust should ultimately rest.

Like many others, I have attempted to avail myself of the many resources God has provided His people to study the original languages of Scripture. Even without the advantage of formally learning Greek and Hebrew, we can accurately determine what the original words were and what they meant. From Strong's Exhaustive Concordance of the Bible, which provides basic word definitions, to the many excellent Hebrew and Greek Lexicons, which provide contextual word definitions, a solid understanding of the original words is obtainable. As a habit when preparing sermons, my first step is to ensure that I understand any textual issues that might exist in the passage. My aim in the early stages of preparation is to ensure I understand as much as possible what the original hearers and readers of Scripture would have understood. Before turning to commentaries, homiletic helps, or any other study resource, my aim is to discover as precisely as I can, the original words of Scripture. The reason this step is necessary is because inerrancy cannot be applied to a translation. God has not called preachers to proclaim the words of human translators; He has called them to proclaim His words. Focused effort should be taken to understand those words with as much precision as possible in support of this calling.

Yet effort in study is not the final, or even the best defense against the concern that translations are not inerrant. The final and best defense is a connection with the Holy Spirit. God inspired the Bible through the working of the Holy Spirit upon human writers, and what this means for us is that we have access to the author of the Bible. I had several college courses where the instructor was the author of the course textbook. There was a great advantage in this because there was no reason for me to not understand the text. I had the final arbiter of its meaning available to me in class if there was a portion of the text I did not understand. In courses where an instructor was teaching from someone else's text, there was always the possibility that both I, and my instructor, might misunderstand the meaning of a portion of the textbook. With the Bible, the Spirit inspired the original words and we therefore have direct access to the Author of the Bible. Far better even than fluency in Hebrew, Aramaic, or Greek, we have the Author who also speaks our language. The Spirit's work can overcome any nuance or apparent discrepancy as we read and study the Bible. Our trust then is not in the written words alone but in God, who wrote the words. The Bible is a book God wrote to man so we can know Him. He did not write it, have men sacrifice their lives in translating it, and call countless preachers to proclaim it, just so that men might know a few facts about Him. He has done these things so that men might come to know Him truly and know Him personally.

The Spirit has always been required to rightly understand God's words. Even those who spoke Greek fluently often misunderstood Jesus even though He was speaking their native tongue. Their misunderstanding was not the result of an inability to understand the words, but from their failure to submit to the Spirit's work within them. Their failure to submit to God through the Spirit barred their understanding. If there is resistance to the work of the Spirit when we study the Bible, our ability to understand what we read will be greatly hindered. Yet we must also guard against a hyper-spiritualism that serves to displace God's word in our lives and churches. The Bible tells us that God does not change (*Jas. 1.17, Heb. 13.8*). The Bible also teaches that the Spirit is the third Person in the Trinity and equal with God. *(Jn. 15.26, Mat. 28.19)* As we have already pointed out, the Spirit inspired the writing of the Scripture. So, we know that what the Bible says is what God say, and God has not changed His mind on what He wrote. The practical and critically important application for us today is that the Spirit will never tell us something contrary to what He has already said in the Bible. Regardless of how passionately we might feel about a subject, and no matter how politically incorrect the teaching of the Bible might become, what the Bible says is what God says. Many false doctrines and much confusion have resulted from the claim that the Spirit has told a person something contrary to Scripture. Paul told the Galatians to be aware of this when he said, "...*if we or an angel from heaven should preach to you a gospel contrary to the one we preached to you, let him be accursed." (Gal 1.8)*

God has made His word available to us, and He has given us His Spirit to guide us in rightly understanding it. While we cannot apply inerrancy to translations of the Bible, we can apply inerrancy to the Spirit Himself. Realizing that the Spirit is the agent that makes the Scripture more than just words on a page (though at the same time not less), our trust and reliance ought always to be in God Himself. We can test our understanding of that which we feel God is telling us by His word and arrive at a reasoned yet spiritually enlightened understanding of God's will. The greatest errors in Christianity often occur when the Bible and the Spirit are divided. The Bible apart from the Spirit is a dead letter that leads to a cold, lifeless rationalism, but the Spirit apart from the Bible pivots toward mysticism and Gnosticism where the feelings, emotions, and opinions of men become the true standard among a people. God is pleased with neither. Further, one error has no real advantage over the other as both end up with men following something other than God Himself. Our adversary does not care which of these paths we choose, and when the enemy of our souls does not care which path we choose, we can be certain that both paths must surely lead to destruction.

Scripture Passages on Inerrancy

I mentioned previously that the inerrancy of Scripture represents a key battleground if we desire to maintain a hold on the anchor of God's word in our lives. We have seen many forsake this anchor and toss it aside while still maintaining that they are Christian. One denomination after another is abandoning the long-held position that the Bible is God's inerrant word. The following passages have been provided to allow the Bible to speak for itself on this topic.

"Every word of God is pure. He is a shield unto them that put their trust in him." (Pro 30.5)

"The words of the Lord are pure words. As silver tried in a furnace of earth, purified seven times." (Ps. 12.6)

"God is not a man, that he should lie; Neither the son of man, that he should repent. Hath he said, and shall he not do it? Or hath he spoken, and shall he not make it good?" (Num 23.19)

"Sanctify them through thy truth. thy word is truth." (Jn 17.17)

"In hope of eternal life, which God, that cannot lie, promised before the world began;" (Tit. 1.2)

"That by two immutable things, in which it was impossible for God to lie, we might have a strong consolation, who have fled for refuge to lay hold upon the hope set before us." (Heb. 6.18)

"And now, O Lord God, thou art that God, and thy words be true, and thou hast promised this goodness unto thy servant." (2 Sam. 7.28)

Reconciling these verses with a view that the Bible is not inerrant would require interpretive gymnastics that no honest reader of the Bible would be willing to perform. These Scriptures tell us that all that God says is true and without error, and to believe the Bible is anything less than inerrant is to disbelieve the Bible. To disbelieve the Bible is to disbelieve God. One who does not believe God is surely not a Christian.

Inerrancy Essential

It will surely be offensive to those who reject the inerrancy of Scripture yet claim to be Christian to be labeled non-Christian. There is a desire to claim Christianity yet deny that the Bible is inerrant. However, it is not possible to be a Christian in the true sense of the word while denying the inerrancy of Scripture. To be a follower of Christ, one must deny himself and follow the Lord. To follow the Lord requires belief in what He said and obedience to what He commanded. When we reject the inerrancy of the Bible, it becomes necessary for us to determine which parts of the Bible are true and which parts are untrue. Men make these judgments, which places man in the seat of authority, and not Christ. Where Christ is not the authority, there is no true Christianity.

If we consider any part of the Bible untrue, then we introduce doubt about the entire Bible. Unanswerable questions arise.

"Which parts of the Bible are true and which parts are not?" "Who can determine the parts of the Bible that are true and the parts that are not?" "If God lied in the first two chapters of Genesis about how He created the world, did He also lie in chapter three about how man became a sinner?" "If God lied about how man became a sinner, did He lie about how a man can be saved?"

One question after another is raised without an authoritative way to answer any of them. These questions show the dangers inherent in rejecting the essential doctrine of Biblical inerrancy. Thomas Jefferson was once seen cutting out portions of his Bible.

When asked what he was doing, he replied, "*I'm cutting out the parts I don't like.*" This is what many continue to do today, if not in statement, they do so in practice. They cut out the sections of the Bible they feel are too offensive, or the parts they believe to be untrue, but if we cut out a single passage and label it untrue, we might as well throw the entire Bible away because that is what we have essentially done, and what we will eventually do, anyway.

Inerrancy and Biblical Interpretation

Correct Biblical interpretation is a skill that every child of God should seek to learn and improve. One of the great joys of the Christian life is the ability to dig deeper into God's word as the years go by and our spiritual wisdom and insight are enhanced as we grow in our understanding of Scripture. The continual study of the Bible causes God's word to flow through our lives and we become more like Christ in our thoughts, words, and deeds. The Scriptures season our communication with God in prayer, and our conversations with friends, family, and coworkers. Events small and great bring Scripture to our minds over the course of an average day. Our spiritual maturity can be measured by how Biblical our thinking has become since the day we were saved.

We must realize, however, that growing in Christ through His word requires effort and skill. It does not happen by default. We will not become mature Christians if we lack the discipline to be daily in the word, or the competency to rightly discern its message. Keeping in mind the necessity of the Holy Spirit mentioned earlier, the right interpretation of the Bible requires certain skills which must be learned and sharpened over time. These skills are not reserved for the pastor or seminary student, but are within the grasp of every child of God.

There are many books that cover the art and science of Biblical interpretation. The existence of these books shows that the Bible is unlike any other book and brings its own interpretive requirements. This is true for the Bible as a whole, and it is also true for the individual books and genres in the Bible. Each type of literature found in the Bible has its own set of requirements for correct interpretation. There are overarching rules of interpretation common to all the books of the Bible, but there are also unique rules of interpretation for each genre of Scripture.

Besides the differences in genre, certain passages of Scripture should be interpreted literally while others should not be. Opinions about when the Bible speaks literally and when it does not is at the heart of many disagreements in interpretation. The Bible speaks literally most of the time, but there are important exceptions when the Bible uses metaphors, analogies, and parables. Significant differences of opinion result when one person reads a verse literally, and another does not. The literal millennial reign of Christ on the earth for one thousand years is a prime example of the significant doctrinal differences that arise when portions of the Bible are read literally or figuratively. These differences do not always strike at the heart of the Gospel and there is room for disagreement between competing opinions among Christian people, but in other cases, the central message of the Gospel is altered to the point that division becomes unavoidable.

The child of God should strive to improve their skills of interpretation as a matter of submission to Christ. We should also improve our understanding of Scripture because of the great damage done when false doctrine goes unchecked in the church, or in our homes. I have heard Christians say, "*I'm not a Bible scholar.*" I realize Christians frequently say this in humility, but the Christian has been called to be precisely that, a scholar (or student) of the Bible. The Bible is a book that requires interpretation, and the effort to correctly interpret the Bible comes down to the work done to ensure that we understand God's intended meaning in the text. A popular approach to group Bible study involves the reading of a portion of Scripture after which the leader asks what the passage means to the people taking part in the study. This can be helpful, but the first and much more important question to answer is what God meant by what He said. Only after understanding what God meant will we be in a right position to understand what it ought to mean for us individually.

The requirement to interpret Scripture has a significant impact on the doctrine of Inerrancy, and even the best Bible scholars are susceptible to misinterpretation. One can study the Scripture with a sincere and honest heart and bring to bear all the right tools of interpretation. They can do all of this and still arrive at an incorrect interpretation of the Bible. The law of non-contradiction makes this reality undeniable since there are so many different beliefs among people all of whom claim to base their teaching on the Bible. One man reads the Bible and comes away with a Calvinist view of salvation. Another reads the same Bible, indeed the very same verses, and comes away with an Arminian view of salvation. One man reads the Bible and comes away with the opinion that Jesus was *part* man and *part* God. Another reads the same Bible and comes away with the opinion that He was *all* man and *all* God. One man reads the Bible and believes Jesus will reign on the earth in a future millennial kingdom *before* the final judgment. Another reads the same Bible and sees the thousand years of Revelation chapter twenty as figurative and believes that the millennial kingdom refers to the present church age.

Do these contradicting interpretations invalidate the doctrine of Inerrancy? Do disagreements over the Bible's message mean that the Bible contains contradictions and errors? No. The Bible is always inerrant, but the same cannot be said of our interpretations. We must remember then that our interpretation of Scripture is not Scripture. The Bible is not subject to you or me but rather we are subject to the Bible. We must read daily, study diligently, and pray that God would help us arrive at a right understanding, but we must not correlate the inerrancy of the Bible with the inerrancy of our interpretation. To do so risks pride setting up in our heart and blinding our eyes to the truth of God's word when our opinion needs correcting. Sometimes, we just get it wrong in our interpretations. Thankfully, God is merciful and does not cast us aside when our understanding is not yet complete or perfect.

The Lost Anchor

How we handle the inevitable differences of opinion that arise between individuals and churches is important. Our goal should always be to discover the meaning of Scripture, and never to simply prove ourselves right. Jesus did not commission us to make disciples *like us*. He told us to make disciples that would become *like Him. (Mat. 28.19-20)* Yet in too many instances, personal identities and the justification for the separate identities of churches and denominations are the primary aim rather than a desire to rightly interpret Scripture. Bearing in mind that the Bible is without error, and we are not, can serve as a solid defense against the religious pride that can so easily separate one believer from another. There are doctrinal issues about which the Bible speaks plainly and are so fundamental to the message of the Gospel that there is no room for compromise. The fundamental tenets of Christianity should never be forsaken for a popular, yet misguided sense of ecumenicalism. Yet the convictions that drive division between Christian people should derive from an honest study of Scripture, and not our personal preferences, denominational customs, identities, or traditions. The reason for this once again, is because it is the Bible, and not man, that is inerrant.

Chapter 12 - The Necessity & Sufficiency of Scripture

"And the tempter came and said to Him, "If You are the Son of God, command that these stones become bread." But He answered and said, "It is written, 'MAN SHALL NOT LIVE ON BREAD ALONE, BUT ON EVERY WORD THAT PROCEEDS OUT OF THE MOUTH OF GOD.'" Matthew 4:3–4

The Necessity of Scripture

It is possible to agree with everything written to this point about the *Authorship*, *Authority*, *Selection*, and *Inerrancy* of Scripture, and still lose our hold on the anchor of the Bible. In addition to holding to the doctrines previously reviewed, we must also maintain a correct view of the *Necessity* of Scripture. One can believe the Bible is without error but believe it to be unnecessary for their lives. It is also possible that one could believe God is the author of the Bible while not seeing its necessity. The denial of the necessity of Scripture is rarely made explicitly, and few Christians would openly admit to holding such a belief. But many unwittingly confess this view through a general lack of knowledge of what the Bible says. Surely our convictions regarding the necessity of the Scriptures would be made most clear by our knowledge of what they say, but the significant Scriptural illiteracy among many professing Christians shows the lost hold on the view that the Bible is necessary. The pressure exerted by society to reject absolute truth has encouraged many churches to see the Bible as a *helpful addition* to the Christian faith, rather than see it as the *foundation* of the Christian faith. A Bible that is considered unnecessary is a Bible that few will read, and the view of the Bible as unnecessary has been a significant contributor to our lost hold on the anchor of Scripture.

The Necessity of the Old Testament

Some believe the Old Testament became unnecessary with

the coming of Christ and the completion of the New Testament. They contend that since we are no longer under the Old Testament Law and are instead under the New Covenant of grace, then the Old Testament is no longer required. However, the promises found in the New Testament become meaningless without the context of the Old Testament. The New Testament speaks of eternal life and salvation through Christ, but apart from the fall of man as recorded in Genesis chapter three, from what exactly are we saved? Are we saved from our bad habits? Is our salvation meant to smooth our life *in* this world, or is it intended to deliver us *from* this world? The New Testament speaks of the prophecies fulfilled in Christ, but how can we determine the veracity of these New Testament claims without the record of the Old Testament? If the Old Testament is no longer necessary, why did Paul state that it was written as an example for us today? *(1 Cor. 10.11)* The New Testament separated from the Old Testament presents a solution to an undefined problem and makes claims disconnected from the context in which those claims were made.

It is not popular to declare what the Old Testament says about a man in his fallen condition. The unwillingness to see man as he truly is before God (apart from salvation in Christ) lies at the root of why many avoid the Old Testament, but the message of salvation is robbed of its strength and power when sin is not confronted. The preaching of salvation apart from the reality of sin is empty preaching. God did not send His Son to a fallen world to suffer and die on our behalf to simply smooth the rough edges of our lives, and Jesus is not a Savior whose intentions are to merely help us salvage our relationships, finances, and good health. Jesus did not endure the intense agony of the cross and lay down His life so that our self-esteem would be lifted. He came to a fallen world in desperate need of a Savior - a Savior from sin. The Old Testament presents one account after another of man's lostness, weakness, and sinfulness. Beginning in Genesis chapter three the Bible confronts us head on with man's sin. We are told that the consequence of sin is death under the judgment of a righteous and holy God, and the close of the Old Testament points to a *continuation* of the story, not a *conclusion* to the story. The New Testament is the realization of the new covenant between God and man -- A covenant of grace and not works. The covenant of grace (the New Testament) is the answer to man's inability to satisfy the covenant of works (the Old Testament). The New Testament, separated from the Old Testament, is an answer to a question that has not been asked.

The Necessity of Scripture & Witness of Creation

Man understands through the observation of the world around him that there is a God. *"The heavens declare the glory of God; And the firmament sheweth his handywork." (Ps 19.1)* To deny a creator demands a belief that the universe originated from nothing. There are only two ultimate choices for explaining life and the existence of the universe. They either came from something (a creator) or they came from nothing. You and I came from something (a creator) or we came from nothing. The acceptance in our society that something can come from nothing represents the height of foolishness. The Bible tells us it is the fool who says there is no God, *(Ps. 14.1)* and surely it is the fool who claims that out of nothing came something (much less everything). Yet this foolishness is called wisdom today. Professors and scientists, in an arrogance coupled with ignorance, postulate one outlandish theory after another to explain how we all got here apart from a creator (God) who put us here.

Though creation bears clear testimony to God, the understanding gleaned from creation that God must exist is not the same thing as understanding the Gospel of Jesus Christ. Some have argued that through creation alone we can come to a saving knowledge of God, but this is not the testimony of the Bible. Acts 4.12 says, *"Neither is there salvation in any other. for there is none other name under heaven given among men, whereby we must be saved."* Looking at the sun reveals that there must be a God, but it does not itself reveal the Son of God. Considering the inexplicable world around us testifies to the rational mind that there must be a God, but it does not show us the Christ who died for our sins. In John 14:6 Jesus says, *"I am the way, the truth, and the life. no man cometh unto the Father, but by me."* The conclusion then is that salvation is only possible through a knowledge of Christ. An acknowledgement of the reality of God that results from an observation of the universe is not the same thing as acknowledging Christ as Lord and Savior. For that, the Bible is necessary. The universe, with full voice sings of its creator *(Ps. 19.1)*, yet it is the Bible alone that reveals who that creator is when we read,

"In the beginning was the Word, and the Word was with God, and the Word was God. The same was in the beginning with God. <u>All things were made by him; and without him was not any thing made that was made.</u>" (Jn. 1.1–3)

Many consider themselves Christian based on their belief in the Bible's claims about the origins of the universe. They recognize that the Christian view of the inception of the universe is the most plausible explanation for how the world came to be. Faced with the choice that out of nothing came everything, or that God created everything, most reasonable people choose the latter. But this belief, by itself, is not the same belief which is necessary for salvation. Salvation involves not only an acknowledgment of God's existence, but an admission of our guilt as sinners before Him. Belief in God's existence is necessary. One can surely not be saved who denies God's existence, yet one must also seek God's forgiveness diligently if he is to be saved. *(Heb 11.6)* Belief that there must be a God is merely the logical conclusion that a reasonable mind infers when the evidence and witness of creation is thoroughly investigated. The immense complexity of the universe simply cannot be explained apart from divine causation. That out of nothing came everything is an idea so preposterous that I believe future generations will look back on our time in amazement over our blindness. Still, salvation requires knowledge provided through the Bible, not just creation.

The Bible itself testifies of the necessity to understand the Scripture to rightly understand the plan of salvation. While glimpses of the Gospel are possible apart from the Bible, seeing it completely comes only through the word of God. The Bible also states that it is necessary to know Scripture to know how to live the Christian life. I said earlier in this book that faith is not blind. A true believer in God comes to a knowledge of God through the working of the Holy Spirit in the mind and the heart. The fuel for the knowledge which the Spirit uses is the truth found in the Bible. The Spirit takes the words of truth from Scripture and guides us to a right understanding of that truth, and truth is a collection of facts and ideas that come from Scripture. The Bible then is the source of the facts of the Gospel. Without it, the facts necessary to understand the plan of salvation and how to live the Christian life are not available. There are reasons that God has so carefully and providentially watched over His word since the moments they were first written, and one of those reasons is the necessity of His word for a lost world to find Him, and for His own people to serve Him.

The Bible is Necessary to Understand the Plan of Salvation

"For whosoever shall call upon the name of the Lord shall be saved. How then shall they call on him in whom they have not believed? and how shall they believe in him of whom they have not

heard? and how shall they hear without a preacher? And how shall they preach, except they be sent? as it is written, How beautiful are the feet of them that preach the gospel of peace, and bring glad tidings of good things! But they have not all obeyed the gospel. For Esaias saith, Lord, who hath believed our report? So then faith cometh by hearing, and hearing by the word of God." (Romans 10.13–17)

Paul states in these verses that hearing (understanding) the word of God is necessary for faith. There are some facts of the Gospel which can be understood apart from the Bible, and one example of this is man's sinfulness. That we are all sinners is self-evident. However, the understanding that death directly results from sin is not immediately apparent. Without the Bible we would not understand that men die because we are sinners. A man does not die because he gets sick. He dies because he is a sinner. Our bodies do not grow weak and our eyes dim as we age because that is just the natural way of things. We do so because these bodies are sinful. The Bible teaches us that death has come into the world because of sin. *(Rom. 6.23)*, but we would not understand this truth without the Bible. Death would never have intruded on life had sin not entered the world, but nothing conclusively ties death to sin through natural observation. The worst sinners frequently live until they are old, and well-behaved children often die in childhood. Only through the word of God do we see the connection between our sin and our inevitable death.

It is through the Bible that we learn that salvation is a narrow gate and a narrow way, *(Mat. 7.14)* but man left to his own understanding would say the opposite. Man would claim that most people are good and deserve to go to Heaven with Hell reserved for only the vilest and most deviant among us, but the Bible tells us the exact opposite. The Bible teaches that our delusional perception of our own righteousness is one of the greatest obstacles to our belief in God and salvation in Christ. It also teaches that only a relative few will find salvation when man would assume that Hell would be for the relative few and Heaven for the remaining many. The promise of Heaven would be unknown to us if we did not discover this truth in the Scripture.

The facts of Jesus' birth, life, death, and resurrection would not be possible apart from the Bible. Nothing in the natural world would point us to the way of salvation through God's giving of His only Son and His death on the cross for our sins. There are no hidden messages in the stars or anywhere else in creation that tell the Gospel story. Only the Bible tells that story. Nothing in creation fully reveals God's plan of salvation for fallen men. Some might argue this point. It might be said that there are many pictures in creation that teach the truths of the Gospel. For instance, some say that the fact that darkness comes every day teaches us that there is an eternal darkness coming for those apart from Christ, and the darkness represents sin and separation. Yet this witness in creation reflects truths gleaned from the pages of Scripture. The dark of night is a visible representation of what we learn from the Bible, and we cannot learn the obvious facts of the

Gospel from creation even if we can sometimes see shadows of those facts in the natural world around us. Without the facts taught in the Bible, the shadows of those facts in creation would never be identifiable because it is the Bible that casts those very shadows. It has pleased God to write a book so we might know the facts of the Gospel and submit to those facts in repentance toward God and faith in the Lord Jesus Christ. *(Acts 20.21)*

The Bible is Necessary to Understand the Christian Life

The Bible is not only necessary to know the facts regarding salvation, it is also necessary to comprehend the facts that relate to living a life that is pleasing to God. I have been asked many times why God placed the Tree of the Knowledge of Good and Evil in the Garden of Eden if He did not want Adam and Eve to eat of its fruit. On the surface, this question points out what appears to be a significant problem for the Christian message and the Bible itself. God is blamed for man's sin and the Christian message is regarded as unfair, but this is not the case at all. God gave Adam and Eve the ability to show their love for Him, and their obedience to Him, by giving them this command. The *ability* to choose the *right thing* is not possible when there is an *inability* to choose the *wrong thing*. Had the tree not been there, then perhaps Adam and Eve would have never done anything *wrong*, but neither would they have done anything *right*. The command of God was a blessing to man. God was not setting Adam and Eve up for failure, He was setting them up for success. That man chose in his freedom to disobey God is not a reflection on God but

is instead a reflection on man.

We love God by keeping His commandments according to John. *(1 Jn. 5.3)*. If there were no commandments to keep, then we could not rightly love God. Obedience to God represents the heart of the Christian life. Christianity is not centered on rituals, traditions, or religious practices, it is centered on loving God. Yet, according to the Scripture, love for God is not merely a subjective matter. It is objective in the sense that loving God involves obedience to His specific commands in the Bible. Loving God is objectively defined through the call to obey what He has prescribed in the Bible.

It is sometimes said of a person who is living in open and unrepentant rebellion against God that they still love Him. It is further claimed that no one can see into another person's heart, and despite the open disobedience in a person's life to what God has commanded, they declare that they still love Him. We cannot understand all the complexities of the human heart. We cannot even know our own hearts with complete certainty. *(Jer. 17.9)* Yet Jesus said that our hearts are not as hidden as we would like to believe them to be. Jesus said that a man's heart is inextricably linked to his treasure. *(Matt. 6.21)* If we want to know what a person loves, we need only look at what they treasure. When a person openly defies the commands of God, they are treasuring their own desires above the desires of God. Their own will is cherished above the will of God. That type of life is not a life governed by love for God, and it reveals a heart that does not love Him. At least, not in the moments of sin and not in a life that has a continual pattern of sin and disobedience to God.

Even those who love God sin. John tells us that if we think we are without sin, we are a liar and deceive ourselves, *(1 Jn 1.10)* but those who love God have a different reaction to sin in their lives than those who do not. For the one who loves God, their sin will be grievous to them. They will mourn their sinfulness and seek forgiveness and pray for strength to avoid the sin in the future. They will not claim a love for God despite their sin. They will claim a desire to avoid sin and overcome sin in their lives because they love God. The ongoing repentance of a child of God throughout his life represents obedience. If sin will continually accompany us while we remain in these bodies of sin, a fact that the Bible makes clear, then surely ongoing repentance for sin is a demonstration of obedience to God and our love for Him. The one who does not repent and does not desire to be reconciled to God shows that he in fact does not love God. It can at least be said that he loves his sin more than he loves God, and a partial love of God is not the love God has called us to give to Him.

The first of the ten commandments tells us we are to have no other gods before us. *(Ex. 20.3)* Sin that is treasured above God becomes a god of our own making. Both the Old and the New Testaments declare that we are to love God with all our heart, soul, mind, and strength. *(Deut. 6.5, Mk 12.30)* Writing to the spiritually lukewarm church in Laodicea, Jesus said He would rather they be cold or hot, but their lukewarm spiritual condition sickened Him. *(Rev. 3.15-16)* These Scriptures tell us then that a half-hearted, unrepentant, disobedient life is a life that does not contain the radical, all-encompassing love for God that He calls us to possess. The Bible contains the commands God would have us obey in our lives. For these reasons and others, the Bible is necessary for us to know how, and in what ways, we can love Him.

The last phrase in 1 John 5:3, which tells us that God's commands are not grievous, sheds much light on the way we are to love and obey God. Many have the mistaken impression that the Christian life is a life where a person continuously disciplines himself to avoid doing the things he wants to do and forces himself to do the things he does not want to do. This view sees the Christian life as a life spent engaged in a constant battle to do the right thing and be the right kind of person. An inward battle is certainly involved in the Christian life, as the old man of sin rebels against the will of the new man created in the likeness of Christ, but we must not reach the conclusion that the Christian life is a life of bondage to a list of things we are to do and things we are to not do. Those who live out their Christianity in this light often feel unhappy and guilty. They seem to be continuously attempting to atone for their sin and feel little of the freedom found in Christ. Scripture does not inform this distorted view of the Christian life. According to the Bible, the one who rightly loves God and keeps

His commandments does so with a glad heart. He does not look at the commands of God as a burden. He instead realizes that God's commands in the Bible provide him the opportunity to show God that he loves Him. It brings him joy to obey God because he knows it brings God joy for him to do so. He also knows that God's commands are for his benefit and happiness and are not meant to restrict him or bring him sorrow.

The enemy often whispers in the believer's ear that their salvation and their Christian life rests on their own performance rather than on Christ. This lie is attractive to our religious pride because it allows us to feel as though we have earned God's approval. This then leads to an empty formalism and legalism that is absent the true joy and freedom of the Christian life. If this wrong thinking is left uncorrected, it can create pride in entire churches. A spiritual elitism sets up among people who congratulate one another on not being like the world. Their prayers reflect the prayer of the self-righteous Pharisee rather than the humble sinner who understood his only hope was the mercy and grace of God. *(Lk. 18.9-14)* Their pride becomes a wedge between the church and the world which God has called them to reach, and a hindrance to the working of the Spirit of God.

Men would follow this wrong path were it not for the Bible's teaching us otherwise. It is counterintuitive to our fallen human reasoning that God loves us, sent His Son to die for us, longs to have fellowship with us, and does not require of us our own righteousness to gain these benefits. Fallen man thinks surely God expects something great from us for us to gain such unspeakable blessings. Surely, He expects us to live exemplary Christian lives before He will approve of us, but the Bible tells us the exact opposite. We are told that it was while we were yet sinners that Christ died for us. *(Rom. 5.8)* We are also told that before we ever loved God, He loved us. *(1 Jn. 4.19)* Had God not told us these things in the Bible, we simply would not know them. May every child of God pause and thank Him for His word, and the unspeakable and unimaginable treasures we find only within its pages.

The Sufficiency of Scripture

"You, however, continue in the things you have learned and become convinced of, knowing from whom you have learned them, and that from childhood you have known the sacred writings which are able to give you the wisdom that leads to salvation through faith which is in Christ Jesus. All Scripture is inspired by God and profitable for teaching, for reproof, for correction, for training in righteousness; so that the man of God may be adequate, equipped for every good work." (2 Timothy 3.14-17)

"I testify to everyone who hears the words of the prophecy of this book. if anyone adds to them, God will add to him the plagues which are written in this book; and if anyone takes away from the words of the book of this prophecy, God will take away his part from the tree of life and from the holy city, which are written in

this book." (Revelation 22.18–19)

Definition

The Sufficiency of Scripture teaches that the Bible is sufficient to understand the way of salvation and the way of service to God. The essential idea behind the doctrine is that with the Bible alone, we can come to an understanding of salvation, and the right way to serve God after salvation. Most Christian denominations claim to believe in the sufficiency of Scripture, yet many who claim this belief often reveal an opposite opinion through their practice. Their doctrine and Statements of Faith may suggest a belief in the Sufficiency of Scripture, but their practice exposes their reliance on other things in addition to the Bible. The idea that a man can sit with his Bible alone and come to a right understanding of God, and a right and complete understanding of how to serve Him, is becoming less and less common in more and more places. The anchor of God's word, however, is the only and all-sufficient anchor necessary to find God and serve God.

∞

The Difference Between Inerrancy and Sufficiency

We covered the doctrine of the Inerrancy of Scripture in chapter eleven. Inerrancy has to do with the truthfulness of the Bible. Belief in the inerrancy of Scripture is integral to the Christian faith. However, it is possible to hold to the Bible's inerrancy while at the same time rejecting its sufficiency. It is one thing to say that the Bible is without error, but it is another thing to say that it contains all we need to know to find God and follow Him in our lives. Many battles have been fought over the Scripture's inerrancy, and rightly so. Yet I fear that amid the fight for inerrancy we have lost ground on the doctrine of the Bible's sufficiency.

As I grow older and become more acquainted with the tactics of the Adversary, I see that he almost always positions a sizable force on the flanks. With each frontal assault on one doctrine, he has a flanking maneuver prepared against another. I believe he has done this with the doctrines of the Inerrancy and the Sufficiency of Scripture. If he loses the battle for inerrancy, he will strike hard at the doctrine of the Bible's sufficiency. He will give up the ground in our minds that the Bible is inerrant and focus his efforts to gain ground on our hold on the Bible's sufficiency. Should he win this battle, he will have won a decisive victory in the life of the believer, the health of a local church, and perhaps even an entire denomination. As soon as one stops believing in the sufficiency of the Bible, they will seek other sources of guidance. In seeking new sources of guidance, they leave behind the Bible. It is of little practical value to believe the Bible is without error if we also believe that it does not speak to every area of our life. But the Bible does speak to every area of our lives. It gives us hope when we feel hopeless. It tells us what love is, and, equally important, what it is not. It shows us how to be sons, daughters, fathers, and mothers. It provides the foundation for a society based on truth and justice. It reminds us on every page there is more to life than the mundane struggles of our daily lives. It chastises and corrects us when we are wrong and encourages us when we are right. It stabilizes us in an unsteady world, and it shows us how to seek forgiveness and restore our relationships. It teaches us how to honor our employers and treat others with respect, love, and honor. It exhorts us to think of the needs of others before thinking of our own. It calls us to a life of joy, peace, and rest in God in a world that offers none of those things apart from Him. It reveals in vibrant color the majesty, love, and power of God, which are seen in only black and white in the created universe around us. It explains why we are alive and the purpose for all our days. It is the anti-venom for the poisonous lies told to us by the serpent and enemy of our souls. It crushes the proud and exalts the humble. It explains why we feel empty without God. It is, indeed, the anchor of our souls. On and on we could go describing the sufficiency of the Bible and we would never get it a hold of it all. The evidence that much has been lost with reference to the Sufficiency of Scripture is rather plain to see in our day. Parents seek wisdom from the latest best seller to raise their children. Pastors read the new church growth book, hoping to find the magical formula to increase attendance. The preacher proclaiming the word of God in the pulpit is deemed antiquated and insufficient to draw and keep men and women engaged in the church. In all these situations, the problem is not with the Bible's insufficient view of us and the world. The problem is with our insufficient view of the Bible.

Chapter 13 - The Clarity of Scripture

"The law of the LORD is perfect, restoring the soul; The testimony of the LORD is sure, making wise the simple." Psalm 19:7

The doctrine of the Clarity of Scripture teaches that the Bible is a book that we can understand. The Clarity of Scripture stands in opposition to the idea that the Bible is a book that only the highly intelligent or the spiritually elite can grasp. The belief that the average person cannot understand the Bible has often served as a discouragement to reading it, but the Bible states that it is a book that we can, and should, understand. The Bible asserts that every person who desires to comprehend the word of God, and goes about their study in the right way, can gain a right understanding of the Bible's message.

Satan will use any means available to him to keep the Bible out of the minds and hearts of people. He focused for many years on keeping the Bible in a language that few could read, and those efforts were highly effective, even if not ultimately successful. He has used many other tactics as well in his fight to prevent people from knowing what God has said in the Bible. One of his more effective strategies has been to convince people that the Bible is just too difficult to comprehend. Many have never truly read the Bible because they believe it is obscure, confusing, and beyond their ability to understand. As a result, they filter their understanding of the Bible through a pastor, a friend, or perhaps a parent. This filtered Scripture might be better than none, but God intends for each of us to mine the treasures of the Bible for ourselves. Discovery in the word of God is a chief joy in the Christian life. I have again and again found myself in awe of God after reading and studying the word of God. The years have not dulled the edge of the sword of the Spirit, they have only sharpened it with time. Sadly however, many do not sharpen their own understanding of the word of God because they believe it to be a book for religious experts and not the common man. I hope to dispel this commonly held but mistaken belief in this chapter on the doctrine of the Clarity of Scripture.

There is no question that the meaning of certain passages in the Bible does not always lie on the surface of the text, and proper understanding requires study and mental digging. The existence of these portions of the Bible should not discourage us from seeking to understand what the Bible says. A. W. Tozer once wrote, "*I believe that we find the Bible difficult because we try to read it as we would read any other book, and it is not the same as any other book.*"[15] We should be mindful that the Bible is a book that communicates eternal truth, and remember that an eternal God is its author. We should recognize that it deals directly with the many complexities of life and reveals the human heart and the mind of God. The depth and complexities of the subjects covered in the Bible should create in us an expectation that there will be ideas and concepts which will demand our careful reading, study, meditation, and prayer. The Clarity of Scripture does not attest that the Bible is always easy to understand, but it does assert that with correct study and prayer, a right understanding of the word of God is within the reach of anyone who desires to comprehend its meaning. The implications inherent in the idea that man can understand a book written by God is a cause of great concern for the enemy of our souls, and he has assaulted this doctrine with great vigor. These assaults range from the methods used to interpret the Bible, to the effort required to meaningfully study it. I have provided the following sections to serve as a defense against

---

[15] Tozer, A.W., (2008). Man: The Dwelling Place of God: What it Means to Have Christ Living in You (p.23). Wingspread.

a few of the more common attacks on this doctrine.

∞

Allow the Clear to Interpret the Obscure

I covered the *Inerrancy of Scripture* in chapter eleven, and it connects closely with the *Clarity of Scripture*. If the Bible is inerrant, then it will not contradict itself. The law of non-contradiction demands that this be true because it is not possible for two opposite assertions to be true at the same time. Inerrancy provides for the certainty that less clear passages will not contradict passages that are more clear.

The Bible teaches plainly that salvation is by grace through faith in Christ and repentance toward God. *(Acts 20.21, Eph. 2.8, 2 Tim. 1.9)* Passages that may appear to teach something contradictory to this truth should be brought into harmony with these clear statements of Scripture. A classic example is the apparent discrepancy between Paul and James regarding the place of works in salvation. Paul says that our justification before God rests on faith. Yet James *appears* to say the exact opposite.

Romans 3.28 For we maintain that a <u>man is justified by faith apart from works</u> of the Law.

James 2.24 24 You see that a <u>man is justified by works and not by faith alone</u>.

What should we do with these verses? Does the Bible contradict itself in these passages? Are Paul and James at odds in their theology as it relates to the doctrine of justification? Is salvation by faith alone, or are works required?

When we come across passages that appear to contradict one other, we must remember the principle of allowing what is clear to interpret what might be less clear. In the example of Paul and James, it is James' words that strike the student of the Bible as being unclear. The reason for this is that the clear and obvious teaching of the New Testament is that salvation is an unmerited gift not gained by our own righteous works. If we identified all the passages of Scripture that plainly state that salvation is by grace, and then do the same with passages that *appear* to claim it is by our works, many more verses would support the doctrine that salvation is by grace, not works. Because most of Scripture speaks of salvation by grace, we know that we have more study to do when James appears to say the opposite. Our approach should not be to interpret the clear teaching of Scripture in the light of a relatively few passages that seem to contradict that clarity. When the Bible says something repeatedly and plainly, we should not call that teaching into question when we come across a few verses that seem to teach something different. Our approach to reconcile Paul and James should be to examine James more closely. Our method should not be to cast the entire New Testament into doubt because of a few verses in James. To do so would be to allow the obscure to interpret the obvious, and this would be a path to confusion, not clarity.

Studying James with a view to the clear teaching of Scripture that salvation is by grace allows us to uncover that James is speaking of the *works* that *accompany* true salvation. He is not asserting that works *produce* salvation. The point he is making is that true salvation, which comes through faith in Christ alone, produces works in our lives. Salvation is often called a new birth, and this is an excellent way to think of salvation as a new birth is exactly what happens when one comes to true saving faith in Christ. A new birth, though, means a new life. It is not possible to have a new birth without a new life. Even when it is for only a few moments, life always follows birth in the natural world. However, new life is not possible without a new birth. None of us had any part or merit in our natural birth. Yet, each of us determines how we live our lives. In the same way, salvation is a work of God whereby a person is born again, and a new life then begins. This new life results from God's grace alone with no dependence on our works, but once we are born again, God has work for us to do to bring Him glory in our lives. Paul himself reconciles his teaching with James in Ephesians chapter two. There he says,

"For by grace you have been saved through faith; and that not of yourselves, it is the gift of God; not as a result of works, so that no one may boast. For we are His workmanship, created in Christ Jesus for good works, which God prepared beforehand so that we would walk in them." (Eph. 2.8-10)

Salvation is by grace apart from works, but salvation is granted in order that we might do good works to glorify God. This example shows the advantage of allowing the clear teaching of the

Bible to interpret passages that are less clear. If we take the opposite approach and attempt to bring clear passages into agreement with those that are less clear, our interpretation of the Bible will be contradictory, and the unbelieving world will be quick to point out our inconsistencies.

Context is King

The Clarity of Scripture is also at risk when passages of the Bible are taken out of context. A single verse separated from its context can be twisted to mean many things it was never intended to mean. For this reason, the Clarity of Scripture requires an interpretational approach that always considers the context of the passage being studied. We find a notable example of a passage commonly taken out of context in the Sermon on the Mount. In the sermon, Jesus says, *"Do not judge so that you will not be judged."* *(Mat. 7.1)* Many verses have suffered the abuse of being taken out of context, but few more so than this one. When quoted apart from its context, this verse appears to teach that we should never judge. Anyone who has stood for truth knows that doing so can be a difficult task. Standing for truth today often gets one labeled judgmental, and in the eyes of an unbelieving world, a person who judges between right and wrong is a person of the worst sort. It is as though the most objectionable thing that we can do to one another today is to offend each other's feelings and opinions. Man's feelings have filled the vacuum left by the absence of truth.

Not only is the truth no longer in the driver's seat of our nation, it appears to no longer even be in the vehicle. We stopped along the way somewhere and asked the truth to get out. We did this largely to spare our feelings, but we also did it so that our self-esteem might reach ever new heights. This mindset causes people to read Matthew 7:1 *in their own context* rather than the *context of Scripture*, and they do not rightly understand what Jesus was teaching. The context of this verse shows that Jesus was not teaching that we should never judge. Instead, He taught that our judgment ought not be *prejudicial* or *hypocritical*. Just four verses after Matthew 7:1 Jesus said, "*You hypocrite, first take the log out of your own eye, and then you will see clearly to take the speck out of your brother's eye.*" *(Mat. 7.5)* The teaching can be summarized to say that before we judge others, we ought to do the more difficult work of judging ourselves and our own motivations, and then, once we have examined ourselves, we are to judge the actions of others when it is our place to do so. Once we get the beam out of our own eye, we can then see rightly to help remove the speck from our brother's eye. We are not to simply ignore our brother's specks, but we are to make sure we have first dealt with our own beams.

Emphasizing the Chapters and Verse Divisions

We can easily take Scripture out of context when we place too much emphasis on the chapter and verse divisions in the Bible.

Chapter and verse divisions are not part of the inspired text. When the writers of Scripture wrote God's words, they did not divide the writing into the chapters and verses we know today. Chapter and verse divisions came much later. It was not until 1227 A.D. that the Biblical text was divided into chapters by Stephen Langton. It was later still in 1551 A.D when the verse divisions were added by Robert Stephanus. The first complete Bible with chapter and verse divisions was printed in 1555 with an edition of the Latin Vulgate Bible. The chapters and verses have been a great help to the study of Scripture, and they are of particular help when we study the Scripture together, or when a minister takes a reading from the pulpit. The preacher can announce the Scripture he intends to speak from by chapter and verse and those in the congregation can easily follow him as he expounds the word of God. However, as with most tools, the chapters and verses in the Bible can be harmful if they are used incorrectly. We have trained our minds to think a new chapter always begins a new topic, and a new verse stands on its own as an independent thought. This assumption contributes to taking single verses like Matthew 7:1 and hanging entire doctrinal concepts on them. We need to remember, however, that the weightier the doctrine, the more support it needs. The false teaching that Christians should not judge is a doctrine of great weight. It impacts every area of the Christian life. If we believe we are not to judge evil, then we must also believe that we are not to promote good. Approving truth requires us to disapprove of error. I cannot promote honesty without disdaining dishonesty. I cannot affirm a love for children without judging as evil the killing of children not yet born. Accepting error requires us to cast away truth. Judgment is required at every turn. Preaching the hope found in the Gospel and judging sin are two sides of the same coin. You cannot do one without also doing the other. The belief that Christians are not to judge changes the entire Gospel message. It is therefore a doctrine of such significance and weight that a handful of verses alone could never adequately support it. The context of each passage of Scripture should therefore be kept in view throughout the study of the Bible. If we defend a major doctrinal position with only a few passages of Scripture, it is likely that we have taken those verses out of context. The chapter and verse divisions in today's Bible can lead us to making this mistake if we are not careful to avoid it.

A Right Spiritual Disposition

Many attempt to understand the Bible apart from faith in God, but a right spiritual condition is essential to understand the meaning of Scripture. Tozer spoke of this when he said,

"Shakespeare may be enjoyed without penitence; we may understand Plato without believing a word he says; but penitence and humility along with faith and obedience are necessary to a right understanding of the Scriptures."[16]

---

[16] Tozer, A.W., (2008). Man: The Dwelling Place of God:

Attempting to understand the Bible apart from the illuminating work of the Spirit of God is like trying to read a book in the dark. Paul refers to this when speaking of his Jewish brethren in 2 Corinthians. There he writes,

"But their minds were hardened; for until this very day at the reading of the old covenant the same veil remains unlifted, because it is removed in Christ. But to this day whenever Moses is read, a veil lies over their heart; but whenever a person turns to the Lord, the veil is taken away." (2 Cor.3.14-16)

The Pharisees in the New Testament were close readers of the Scriptures, but their lack of faith darkened their understanding. Faith is the light by which we must read the Bible. Faith in Christ removes the veil that prevents the light of understanding from shining into our hearts and minds. The difficulty with our comprehension of Scripture is more often a lack of faith in what we read, more than in an intellectual inability to understand. As we read the Bible, we should keep in mind that we are called *children* of God for a reason. A child trusts what their parent tells them even when the child does not fully understand everything their mother or father says or does. They trust that they are being told the truth because of the trust they have in their parent. Jesus encouraged this childlike trust when He said, *"Truly I say to you, whoever does not receive the kingdom of God like a child will not enter it at all." (Mk. 10.15)* When we come across difficult

---

What it Means to Have Christ Living in You (p.25). Wingspread.

passages, it can aid our understanding to analyze whether our struggle is due to a lack of intellectual understanding, or if it is due rather to a lack of trust in what we are reading.

∞

A Right Mindset

The Bible tells us that God is not a God of confusion but of peace. *(1 Cor. 14.33)* It stands to reason then that the book He has written us is not confusing either. We should never think of the Bible as a book beyond our comprehension. To make this claim comes remarkably close to denying what God has said about Himself. That there are passages in the Bible that can elude our understanding for a time is beyond dispute, and we can wrestle for years trying to understand certain portions of the Scripture. Yet that should not cause us to think of the Bible as a book that cannot be understood. The lack of seeing the clarity of Scripture is often due to the way we approach the study of the Bible. Like a pilot who takes the wrong approach to flying a plane, if we take the wrong approach in our study, we will not arrive safely at our intended destination.

What, then, is the right mindset for studying the Bible? What approach is best to ensure we come away from our study of the Bible with clarity and not confusion? A few thoughts are provided here by way of answer.

∞

Humility

The clarity of Scripture will elude anyone who comes to the Bible with pride. It is the humble person who has access to wisdom and understanding, not the proud. *(Pro. 11.2)* Most people prefer pride over humility, and this is a primary reason so many do not understand the Bible. From our earliest years, we are encouraged to be proud of ourselves. We are proud of our communities, our churches, our schools, and our homes, and all this pride often creates a barrier to our understanding of the Scripture. Our study of God's word must be seasoned liberally and always with humility. We must search the word as one who needs understanding, and not as one who already understands. We must inquire of the Scripture what our position on issues ought to be, rather than use the Bible as a tool to defend already held positions. Studying Scripture involves recognizing that we do not have the answers. In humility, we realize that we often do not even have the right questions. Jesus frequently responded to questions by answering a different question that had not been asked. In these situations, Jesus not only provided the right answers, but He provided the right questions. The Spirit does this for us today when the questions we are asking the Bible are not the right questions, preventing us from gaining understanding.

In John chapter three, Nicodemus came to Jesus and stated his belief that He had come from God. His unstated questions involved the desire to learn more about who Jesus was so he could put the Lord in the context of his existing view of Scripture. Nicodemus' view of himself was that he was righteous because of his genealogical connection with Abraham. His theology centered on the idea that a person was righteous simply because of who they were. If they were a Jew, they were a child of God. If they were not a Jew, then they were not a child of God. Jesus knew this, and His immediate response was to tell Nicodemus about the necessity of the new birth to enter the Kingdom of Heaven. *(Jn 3.3)* Jesus' answer to Nicodemus' unstated questions takes him down a notably different path than Nicodemus originally intended to go. Nicodemus' pride in his Jewish heritage had to be questioned and removed before he could understand who Jesus was and what He was working to accomplish. Until the wall of pride which had been built up in Nicodemus since his childhood was broken down, truth would never penetrate his heart. The same is true for each of us.

Pride is a chameleon sin. It changes colors so effectively that we rarely realize it is present in our lives. It can also alter its shape to appear to the outside world and to ourselves as righteousness. The Pharisee who thanked God that he was not like the publican is one such example. *(Lk. 18.11)* The Pharisee's sincerity is an often-missed reality when we read this passage. We are disgusted at his pride and rightly so, but we should realize that it is unlikely that the Pharisee saw the pride that dripped from his tongue. Pride had dressed itself up in religious piety so effectively that the Pharisee did not see it for what it was. From a distance it is easy for us to see the pride in this man, but the man himself did not see it, just as we often cannot see our own pride when it is obvious to others.

Sermons on the prayers of the Pharisee and the publican frequently focus on the publican's humble prayer for God's mercy. *(Lk 18.13)* The prayer of the publican is a wonderful example of Godly repentance that works salvation. However, we must not miss the danger that religious pride poses as demonstrated by the Pharisee. When we allow pride in our own religious convictions to take the chief seat in our mind and heart, it will limit our ability to understand the Bible. Our belief that we have all the right questions and all the right answers prevents us from further growth in the knowledge of the Scripture. In our pride, we believe that the Bible will always affirm our personal or denominational preferences. We must set aside this deadly religious pride if we desire to see the Bible clearly. If pride results from our study, then we have not rightly studied. A humble heart and a humble mind are indispensable tools in the effort to increase our understanding. A wise man, after study and thought, will change his opinion, but a fool never will. The difference between wisdom and foolishness frequently comes down to a humble willingness to see when our views are not consistent with the truth of God's word and then change them accordingly.

Pride can even dress itself up to look like humility. This manifestation of pride often claims to be simple and unlearned. Overreacting to the academic pride of the modern-day Pharisee, some have erred by rejecting the deliberate and purposeful study of Scripture. They make the claim of a dependence entirely on the Holy Spirit. It is thought that if a preacher does not prepare a sermon and instead gets behind the pulpit with no thought of what he will say, then whatever he says must be from God through the Spirit. While this approach is often considered humble, it is just as often pride showing up in a different form, yet whatever form pride takes, it destroys whatever it touches.

God has called us throughout the Bible to read, study, and get His word into our hearts. *(Deut. 6.6, Ps 119.11)* God calls the Bible a lamp to our feet and a light to our path. *(Ps. 119.105)* Without the Bible then, we know neither where we are (with no lamp to our feet) or where we are going (with no light to our path). Many Christians, and even many churches, resemble people with no clear view of where they are or where they are going. I have heard sermons that caused me to wonder where we started and where we were heading. To my shame, I have given some of those sermons. Humility might be the intent, but there is pride in ignorance as well as learning.

We should certainly reject the pride the Pharisee felt in himself in Luke chapter eleven, but we should not reject the specific things he claimed to be doing. Should we not all strive to differ from other men as followers of God? Surely, we should not be extortioners, unjust, or adulterers. God commands us to give tithes of what He has given us, so surely the Pharisee's tithing was not wrong. Because the Pharisee was proud of his learning and his good deeds, should we reject learning and the doing of good deeds? If study and learning should be rejected because they can

174

lead to pride, what other things should we reject because they too can lead to pride? We will soon find ourselves at a standstill if we remove from our activities anything which can lead to pride. Yet in all our activity, including the study of the Bible, humility will be necessary, or pride will snatch away the benefit we hope to gain for ourselves and others.

∞

A Willingness to Work

The Bible calls us to a willingness to work. Paul says, "*If anyone is not willing to work, then he is not to eat either.*" *(2 Thes. 3.10)* Solomon decries the sluggard and lazy man and encourages him to imitate the continual activity of the ant. *(Prov. 6.6-8)* A strong work ethic is necessary to a healthy Christian life. I have often said that I desire two things for my sons. First, that they possess a Biblical worldview. Second, that they possess a strong work ethic. If I send them from my home with those two qualities, I will not fear for them or for those for whom they will one day be responsible. If I am blessed with future daughters-in-law and grandchildren, they will need husbands and fathers unafraid of, and well acquainted with, hard work.

It is not always understood that studying the Bible requires discipline and hard work. We often attribute an understanding of the Bible to intelligence, or a greater capacity for spiritual discernment, but the more frequent reason that one has understanding, and another does not, is that the first has done the work necessary to understand, while the other has not. Clarity and understanding do not come without diligence in study. Most things in life that are worth doing require effort and understanding the Bible is no exception.

Every four years, we watch the world's best athletes compete in the Olympic Games, and we marvel at their abilities and appreciate the obvious commitment they have made to compete at a world class level. What we do not see are the countless hours spent in preparation. We do not see them turn off their alarm clocks hours before the sun comes up. We do not see them struggle with the aches and pains of years of training that are not televised. There are no crowds to cheer them out of bed when they would prefer to sleep just a little longer. There are no trophies at the end of their training runs, but they understand that there are no trophies without them either. Paul uses the discipline of an athlete to describe the Christian life. He tells us to, "...*lay aside every weight, and sin which clings so closely, and let us run with endurance the race that is set before us*," *(Heb 12.1)* Paul told Timothy to, "*discipline yourself for the purpose of godliness;*" *(1 Tim. 4.7)* The word *discipline* in 1 Timothy 4:7 is translated from a Greek word used to describe the training of an athlete. Among the necessary life disciplines of the Christian life, is the consistent study of the Bible. This study will often include hard work and labor. The establishment of a habit of Bible reading and Bible study does not come without discipline. When a passage of Scripture is discovered where the meaning is not immediately clear, the hard work of discovery and understanding must begin.

Far too often though, we make the excuse that the Bible is too difficult to understand, and we put in little effort to remove the confusion. The problem is not an inability to understand or a lack of intelligence. The problem is an unwillingness to do the work necessary to gain understanding.

We have lost in our world of modern conveniences something of a willingness to work. In few places has this had a more negative impact than on the study of God's word. We want to read the Bible and come away with crystal clear clarity with no more effort than it takes to read the morning news, but surely, we cannot rightly expect this to be the case. The words in the Bible come from the mind of God. We are reading about eternity, salvation, and spiritual things. It simply stands to reason that understanding the Bible will require more from us than simple reading. Do not give up on passages that at first seem unclear. Believe God when He says that the Bible is a book He wants you to understand and set yourself to do the work necessary to discover His meaning. While engaging in the work, never forget that understanding will come ultimately from God, but remember that He has given you a mind. A mind that has been fearfully and wonderfully made. A mind that can read, think, ponder, and discover the truths He has revealed in the Bible. If God gave us our minds, then the discoveries we make with them are only possible because of Him. In this we see that though we put forth effort, understanding is always God's gift, and not our own triumph.

Many have a fear of reason and logic in spiritual things. They believe that too much study turns religion into a cold, lifeless, academic affair. Yet human reason is a gift from God. God did not make us mindless creatures unable to contemplate and comprehend truth. Greater understanding of the truth should never cool the fires of passion for God. Instead, as our knowledge increases so too should our passion, love, and commitment to Him. The more we know God, the more reason we find to bow in humble adoration and praise. Yet increasing our knowledge of God often requires work on our part. So, like the athlete in training, let us discipline ourselves to Godliness through the diligent study of His word. Let us wake before dawn and give ourselves to the hard work of reading, prayer, and the study of Scripture.

A Willingness to Wait

There is another obstacle that can stand in the way of seeing the Clarity of Scripture. That obstacle is an impatience on our part to wait for God to bring clarity at a time of His choosing. When we put ourselves to the hard work of reading and study, we hope that understanding will come quickly, but God's word is not merely a set of principles and truths that can be fully understood separate from experience. As was mentioned earlier, it is one thing to understand that we are to forgive our enemies, *(Mat. 5.44)* and it is another thing to truly forgive them. It is one thing to know that we are to count all the world's treasures as rubbish next to knowing Christ, *(Phil. 3.8)* and it is quite another to set aside the money, fame, and power of this world so that we might truly know Christ. We cannot fully know certain truths in the Bible until they are experienced in our life. When the Bible speaks of knowing, it frequently refers to knowledge that goes beyond the *intellectual* and moves into the *experiential*. When the Bible speaks of a man knowing his wife, it is speaking of knowledge that is deeper than a knowledge of her mere existence. It is speaking of an intimate physical, emotional, and spiritual connection that is only possible through experience. When the Bible speaks of knowing God, it is speaking in the same way. Knowing God is not just a *fact* to be *understood*, it is a *Person* to be *known* and *experienced*. (*2 Tim. 1.12*)

Experience is essential to knowledge, and experience is something that takes place in time. Many lack a clear understanding of the Scripture simply because they have not experienced the truth of the Bible in their lives. Salvation is not understood because they have not experienced the brokenness and guilt of sin. They have not felt for themselves the cords of death wrapping around them because of their sin. *(Ps 116.3)* They might realize that they are sinful people, but the knowledge of what it means to be a sinner in the sight of a just, holy, and righteous God has not been experienced in the heart. Knowing that one is a sinner is one thing. Knowing the conviction that such sin should cause in the heart is another. I fear there are many professing Christians who *know* a lot about the Bible but have *experienced* little of it in their lives. The Bible will forever be just out of their reach so long as their knowledge does not include true experience.

It should also be kept in mind that maturity in the word of God is something which is measured in years and decades, not hours or days. One who has a significant understanding of the word of God is one who has spent many years in careful and consistent study. Two things have conspired together to prevent us from understanding the necessity of time to see the Scripture clearly. The first is the impatience of modern man, and the second is our present obsession with youth.

Far too often as we read the Bible, we are expecting quick understanding. We soon grow discouraged if we do not gain understanding after one or two readings. Unwilling to wait patiently for understanding to come over time, we give up and set aside our Bibles and seek other sources of guidance that require less effort to understand. We prefer that our minister do our reading, thinking, and studying for us and then give us his cliff notes in his weekly sermons. This might take far less effort and far less time, but it also ends in far less understanding. Our disposition toward the word as we study should be one of great patience and a willingness to seek clarity over many years of ongoing study.

The present-day obsession with youth is also a frequent hindrance to seeing the Clarity of Scripture. Our culture celebrates youth and dismisses the aged. We give more weight to the opinions of the young star in Hollywood than the opinions of men and women who have come to far greater understanding of life through years of experience and study. Christianity is not immune from this tendency of man, and we often prefer the new fair-haired preacher in his youth over the gray-haired servant who has been beaten and battered by years of ministry. The older man might not strike as pleasing a pose, but his understanding and knowledge of God and His word are likely greater than his younger brother's. This is not to say that young ministers cannot possess knowledge, but the obsession with youth can sometimes serve as a hindrance to recognizing that hard work, patience, time, and experience are all necessary ingredients to maturity in God's word.

∞

A Willingness to Obey

The Clarity of Scripture frequently eludes those who have a disobedient heart toward God. God has called us to obey and to submit completely to His will in our lives. An unwillingness to obey God is often accompanied by a claim to be uncertain about the meaning of a command of God in the Bible. The root cause of our misunderstanding in these cases is a lack of obedience, not a lack of intelligence. We do not miss the clarity of the Bible because a passage of Scripture is difficult to understand -- we miss it because obedience is difficult and we choose to disobey. We often call our lack of obedience confusion, but it is disobedience all the same. James tells us,

"...to one who knows the right thing to do and does not do it, to him it is sin." (Ja. 4.17) Jesus said, *"If anyone wishes to come after me, he must deny himself, and take up his cross daily and*

follow me." (Lk 9.23)

This call of Christ is a call that is easy to understand. To follow Christ is to forsake our own will. To follow Christ is to bear the cross He gives us every day of our lives. It is to love God more than we love ourselves. It is to love Jesus more than we love anyone or anything else. A Christian is someone who has turned completely from the things of the world. To be a friend of God is to be an enemy of the world. (*Jam. 4.4*) These may not be easy commands to obey, but they are simple commands to understand. It is difficult to live as a Christian in this world and it seems to be getting more difficult with each passing day in our country, but we must not classify an *unwillingness to obey* as an *inability to understand*. It will not serve to claim confusion of mind when the issue is rebellion of heart. God frequently brings specific things to our minds as we read Scripture that shed light on how we should make specific decisions in our lives. Decisions about who we should marry, where we should live, what job we should choose, how we spend our money or how we invest our free time. These and all the other issues of life are to be determined in light of a complete submission to God. The clarity of Scripture then ties directly to our willingness to obey what it says. A disobedient heart will almost always lead to a confused mind.

Clarity a Cause for Praise

The Bible's clarity is a cause for us to give praise to God. He has given us a book that tells us who He is, and He has made that book understandable. This can only mean that God wants us to know Him. If He desired to hide Himself from us, then surely, He would never have written us a book in the first place. Had He desired to make Himself known to only the highly intelligent or a select few, then surely, He would have written a book that would have been understandable by only those few. But this is not the case. God has written a book for us all.

It is sad and unnecessary to feel intimidated by the Bible. Intimidation should not be our view of Scripture. Meditating on the word of God should be the delight of our life. The Psalmist identifies the blessed man as the one who thinks about and ponders God's words day and night, *(Ps. 1.1-2)* but men rarely meditate on a book that they feel is beyond their ability to understand. We have pointed out a few obstacles to the Clarity of Scripture in this chapter. If you have struggled to understand the Bible, I encourage you to review these obstacles with an honest mind and heart. Clear away the obstacles in the path of your study and you will find that greater progress will be made.

If you have been called to preach the word of God, encourage your hearers with the truth of the Scriptures clarity. Do not discourage your hearers from studying and seeking understanding on their own by inferring that you have some secret ability or special blessing of God to unlock the meaning of the Bible which they do not possess. This type of thinking is dangerously close to the reality that many people lived under when only the clergy could read the Bible. An imbalance of understanding between the pulpit and the pew is always a sign that trouble is on the horizon. The Clarity of Scripture is a defensive wall against the spiritual abuse that always follows when one group of people are thought to possess a greater ability to understand God's word than another. When a *chosen few* are considered to have a higher ability to understand God's word than the *common person*, it will not be long before those chosen few will usurp the Bible as the final arbiter of truth. Whether maliciously or through the best of intentions, men will become followers of men and not God. The Clarity of Scripture is a strong defense against spiritual tyranny and abuse. Of all the doctrines that relate to the Bible, the Clarity of Scripture is perhaps the least understood. As we have seen however, it is a crucial doctrine with which we must all be familiar if we are to restore and maintain our hold on the anchor of the Bible.

Part Three

Restoring the Anchor

Chapter 14 - The Application to Life

"'I am the LORD your God; walk in My statutes and keep My ordinances and observe them." Ezekiel 20:19

<u>Introduction to Part Three</u>

I called attention to the lost anchor of truth in our nation, and pointed to several signs that reveal we are no longer securely tied to the truth of the Bible in Part One. In Part Two, fundamental doctrines about the Bible were reviewed so that we might recognize once again the key characteristics of the anchor of Scripture. However, realizing we have lost the anchor is merely the first step. The next step is to find a solution to the problem. It would be of little practical benefit to diagnose a disease without prescribing a treatment for that disease. In the same way, it would be of little value to point out our disconnection from the Bible without identifying ways to restore it once again, but even the identification of solutions alone will still not be enough to correct the problem. There is a final step we must take. That final step is to implement the solutions identified. The final chapters of this book offer a beginning point for how the anchor might be restored, and an encouragement to make the necessary changes in our lives so that the anchor might be truly recovered.

The removal of the Bible as the anchor of our nation is clear to anyone who is paying attention to the drifting from truth our country has experienced. Most Christians who desire to walk in the ways of God see this problem daily, and this is a good thing. If the problem were unseen, the solutions to the problem would remain forever hidden. Yet many still do not see the problem. I am often bewildered by Christians who appear to be blind to the spiritual devastation that has taken place over the past few decades in our nation. Surely this is evidence that there is little prayer, little meditation, little consideration, and little critical thinking about the world they are living in. They are like the Jews who stayed behind in Babylon after they were given the opportunity to return home to Israel. The ease and comforts in Babylon were just too much to give up in order to return home to Israel. There is little hope of restoring the anchor of the Bible among those who either do not see, or refuse to see, the absence of the Bible in our nation as the serious problem it represents. Perhaps they believe that hearing a sermon from a preacher on Sunday is all the Bible they need. Or maybe they think their Christianity is separate from their day-to-day activities, making the Bible unnecessary for most of their lives. My prayer is that God will open their eyes so they might see just how much they are drifting in life without the Bible to hold them through all of life's challenges and opportunities.

Sermons, articles, and books that point out problems without attempting to offer solutions are easy. Offering solutions is where the difficulty most often really begins. Identifying problems while preaching will often garner many more "*Amen's!*" from the crowd than suggestions of specific solutions. When a pastor states that we are not reading our Bibles enough, most will quickly agree. When the pastor offers the solution of substituting an hour of Netflix for an hour of Bible reading each day, the eagerness in the pew sees a marked decrease. When a preacher claims that our nation has gone astray and departed from God, there is little disagreement or debate. Yet, when the church is reminded that they are the salt of the earth and it is their responsibility to season the world with God's word, the "*Amen's*" are much quieter. We must not be guilty of merely identifying problems without doing the much more difficult work of searching God's word to find solutions to those problems.

Yet, there is still more to do after seeing the problem and identifying the solution. This final work is the most difficult of the three. Once we see the problem and identify a solution, we must *implement* the solution. Once we realize that there is not enough time in our day given to reading God's word, and understand that sacrificing one hour of Netflix helps to solve the problem, we must then in reality sacrifice that hour of entertainment and replace it with an hour of reading our Bibles. This principle holds true for us individually, as well as in the larger discussion of the lost anchor of the Bible in our nation. There are things which we must do if we desire to restore it to its rightful place.

Satan will marshal an appropriate amount of resistance at each step along the path of restoring the Bible as the anchor of our lives. He places many distractions in our lives to keep us from ever seeing the problem in the first place. If he cannot keep us from seeing the problem, he will then call upon greater forces to keep us content in seeing the problem. He will encourage our pride and tempt us to think we are better than others because we see the problem where others do not. If we do, however, make it to the point of identifying solutions, Satan will summon all the strength at his disposal to see that we do not implement those solutions. This is his final stand and he knows it. The gap between identifying the solution and implementing the solution is a spiritual demilitarized zone between us and our enemy. Once we identify a solution to the removal of the Bible from our lives and attempt to carry out that solution, we will find ourselves engaged in a life and death struggle. The stakes in this struggle are Heaven and Hell for the eternal souls of men and women. The battle will be fierce, and the costs will be high. The enemy will frighten and alarm. Fellow soldiers will be struck down, and others will willingly lay down their arms. In the hour of our most desperate confrontation with the adversary, we must pray that God would open our eyes, and the eyes of those around us, to see that those who are with us are more than those who are against us. *(2 Ki. 6.15-17)* We must press on in the battle even if the fight costs us our comforts, earthly treasures, or even our lives.

While Head of School at Coram Deo Academy, I once wrote of the battle we were engaged in as a Christian school. A parent wrote to me concerned about my use of the allusion to a fight and felt my language was antagonistic. This parent's letter was sincere and was sent with honest intentions. Yet there is no other way to describe the Christian life than a battle. Paul spoke of the Christian life as a battle many times. *(2 Tim. 2.3, Eph. 6.11, 1 Tim. 6.12)* Each time I read a bumper sticker that says, "*War is not the answer.*" I am reminded that many consider the absence of conflict to be the definition of peace. So long as no one is openly fighting, then all is thought to be well. This view places the absence of struggle as the most important thing, but many people throughout history have been subjugated, ill-treated, and oppressed in the very midst of otherwise peaceful circumstances. The absence of struggle in the Christian life is often not the indicator that things are going well. It is far more often an indicator that we have lost the battle in which we were once engaged.

190

Part three of this book is an attempt to identify solutions and encourage us to implement those solutions in our lives. I realize that these solutions will meet with resistance. I understand that implementing these solutions is nothing less than a call to arms. I know that Satan will take notice and send his armies to stop the progress. But I also know that seeing the problem is not enough. Seeing solutions is not enough. We must make the actual changes in our lives, our homes, and our churches that are necessary to restore the anchor of God's word once again. Anything less than this will simply never be enough.

We have arrived at a pivotal point in our nation's history. We have lost the anchor of the Bible in most facets of public life. The Scriptures are given no place in the public education of the nearly 50 million young people in our nation. Many of these young people will grow up to occupy important places in society. Most of tomorrow's leaders are in classrooms today where the Bible is dismissed and criticized if it is even mentioned at all. The position and policies of our government no longer acknowledge God and His word. Even many religious organizations and denominations have detached themselves from the anchor of God's word. Most people today no longer believe what I have said about the Bible in this book. So, what should we do? What should those who continue to believe the Bible do about this problem? Should we pull away from our society where it is getting more difficult to hold to our convictions about God and His absolute truth? Or should we compromise our beliefs to gain the acceptance of the world? How we answer these questions will determine the path forward.

∞

Remain Engaged with the World

The Christian experience in the United States has been the exception to the historical rule. Most of history has seen the Christian openly persecuted for his trust in God and his belief in the Bible. For most Christians in the United States, however, little persecution has attended their lives. Persecution is increasing in our land, but it has not yet come close to the level faced by our spiritual forefathers. In November 2012 I was preaching on the radio at a station just outside of Monrovia Liberia. Guards were posted at the gates of the station to watch for those who would come to disrupt the broadcast and bring harm to those of us who were engaged in the work. That night I gained a new appreciation for the fact that the gates of Heaven will never be shut because there will be no threat of harm there. *(Rev. 21.25)* I have not once attended a church in the United States where I felt even a slight fear for my safety or that of my family. I would never wish open persecution on anyone. Yet, the lack of persecution comes with its own dangers.

I mention persecution because it will impact our thinking regarding what we should do about the lost anchor of the Bible in our nation. Some will feel a pull to close themselves off from the world to avoid the inevitable persecution that will follow. Some have already made this decision and have retreated from the world. Their unwillingness to forsake their belief in the Bible is commendable, but I must point out that the very Bible they desire to follow calls for them to be *in* the world. In the great prayer of Christ found in John chapter seventeen, Jesus prays for His followers and says,

"I have given them Your word; and the world has hated them, because they are not of the world, even as I am not of the world. I do not ask You to take them out of the world, but to keep them from the evil one. They are not of the world, even as I am not of the world." (Jn. 17.14–16)

We should note that Jesus prays specifically that His followers would not be taken out of the world. He did not desire that His people pull away from the world and live secluded lives. To do so would have been the *easier* path, but it would not have been the *right* path. The Jews who came to Christ in the first century were rejected and persecuted greatly by their fellow Jews. The Gentile believers faced persecution by the Jews and their fellow Gentiles. Jesus knew that His people would be tempted to remove themselves from the world to escape persecution and so He prays that they would not do so.

Why would Jesus make this request of His Father? Why would He want His people to face persecution rather than avoid it? He gave the answer earlier in His ministry. He told His followers that they were the light of the world. *(Mat. 5.14)* The entire purpose of a light is to shine in darkness. The Christian then is to be a light in the spiritual darkness of this world. He is not to run away from the darkness of the world. He is to bring light to that darkness. When those who believe that the Bible is God's inerrant word remove themselves from the world, they remove the light that such belief would bring to a humanity lost in darkness. We must not respond to the removal of the anchor of God's word by removing ourselves from the world. We are to remain engaged in the battle. We must face the persecution that our belief in God's word will bring. We must ever trust that God will providentially watch over our lives and will lead us safely home to Him regardless of the difficult paths that we must walk on this brief side of eternity.

This engagement must be with those who openly reject Christianity as well as those who may claim to be Christian but reject the historical doctrines that have been held about the Bible. There is a white field of harvest in church pews across our nation. People lost in a relative Christianity anchored to nothing but the relative statements of men. Satan does all he can to ensure that light does not reach the darkness in which he works, and nowhere is he more active than in churches across our nation. If those who hold to the truth of the Bible remove themselves entirely from those lost in religious darkness, how will those people ever see the light? It is one thing to hold tightly to the core doctrines of Christianity. It is another to allow rigid sectarianism to separate those who have light from those who are close to losing what light remains, and those who have begun to wander in open darkness.

Religious sectarianism often finds itself answering questions that no one lost in the darkness is even asking. We must take care that we do not conflate allegiance to a denomination with allegiance to doctrine or allegiance to God. A study of many of the major denominations in the United States reveals that many no longer believe what they once believed. Over time, allegiance to a denomination usurped allegiance to God. The corruptive seeds of this misplaced allegiance have born the fruit of division, strife, and churches untethered from the unchanging word of God. My prayer is that all those who continue to hold to the inerrancy, necessity, and sufficiency of the word of God will not hide behind their church walls but will instead engage fully with a world in desperate need of the light which they possess. Ever watchful against error, but ever hopeful to gain a brother.

Learn and Live. Applying the Word to Life

Jesus was once asked which commandment in the Scripture was the greatest. His answer was that we are to love God with all our heart, soul, strength, and mind. *(Lk. 10.27)* There is enough in this one sentence of the Lord to keep us busy with applying Scripture to our lives were we to live for a thousand years. There is no lack of opportunity for the application of Scripture. What is often lacking, however, is our willing, thoughtful, and purposeful effort to apply God's word to our lives. To *live* what we *learn*. To turn knowledge into wisdom through experiential obedience in the lives we have been given. To experience God's faithfulness by standing on the promises He makes. To realize that when we stray from His path, we, and those around us will all suffer.

∞

We have all heard the phrase, *"Live and learn."* There is a degree of unavoidable truth to this statement. As I called out in the chapter on the Clarity of Scripture, there are some things that we must experience firsthand before we can fully understand them, but a potential danger lurks in this advice. Far too many Christians have adopted an exclusive live and learn approach to following God. The idea seems to be that if God wants them to know something, He will intervene and let them know what He wants them to know without their active effort to learn His will. But the Bible does not encourage a live and learn approach to discovering God's will for our lives. The Bible calls for us to first learn and then live. In Deuteronomy chapter six, the Israelites were told to lay hold of the commands of God and teach them diligently to their children. They were told,

"These words, which I am commanding you today, shall be on your heart. You shall teach them diligently to your sons and shall talk of them when you sit in your house and when you walk by the way and when you lie down and when you riseup. You shall bind them as a sign on your hand and they shall be as frontals on your forehead. You shall write them on the doorposts of your house and on your gates." (Deut. 6.6–9).

This passage is one of the clearest calls in Scripture to teach children the commands of God before they go out on their own. God does not encourage Israel to venture out in their lives and trust that He will teach them what they need to know when they need to know it. They were to be diligent to hide God's word in their own hearts, and then teach their children what God had said. The spiritual walls of many families and churches have been broken down today because this command has not been obeyed. Many have turned over the education of their children to the world, and the average youth today knows precious little about the Bible. Without the knowledge of the Bible to inform them of how they ought to think, feel, and behave, these young people learn lessons the hard way when the consequences of sin follow their poor choices in life.

God's call for Israel to teach their children His commands came with a purpose. God does not command men to obey Him simply to watch them obey. He commands them to obey because He loves them, and He knows what is best for them. He knows the path that leads to blessing and He knows the path that leads to ruin. In Deuteronomy chapter six God goes on to say,

"Then it shall come about when the LORD your God brings you into the land which He swore to your fathers, Abraham, Isaac and Jacob, to give you, great and splendid cities which you did not build, and houses full of all good things which you did not fill, and hewn cisterns which you did not dig, vineyards and olive trees which you did not plant, and you eat and are satisfied, then watch yourself, that you do not forget the LORD who brought you from

the land of Egypt, out of the house of slavery." (Deut. 6.10–12).

After God gives the command in verses six through nine, verse ten begins with, *"then"*. The command to obey does not come without a *reason* for the command. They were to instruct their children so that they would know how to serve God once He had brought them to the land of promise. Throughout the Bible, the pattern is to first learn and then live. It is not to live and then learn. We are to read the Bible and learn what God has to say about life and then apply God's word to our individual lives. Retaking this approach to life will be key to restoring the anchor of the Bible.

There are moments during the preparation and delivery of sermons that I wonder if we should move past the first point of the message until we all go away and think about how our lives should be changed due to the implications of the first point. If we took only one lesson from the weekly sermons we hear and intentionally pray and strive to conform our lives to that one point, it would dramatically change our lives in short order. We do not need to *hear* something new nearly so much as we need to *live* something new. The lives of unbelievers would be powerfully impacted as well when we bring light to the darkness of their world. Many lost in darkness do not realize the depth of the darkness that shrouds their lives. It is not until someone comes into their lives who possesses the light of God that the extent of their own darkness is revealed. The light of the believer in God will illuminate the darkness around them when they live honestly and act with integrity as they perform their jobs, raise their children, pay their bills, and go about their day-to-day activities.

The amount of spiritual light in a nation depends on the degree to which God's people are applying God's word to their own lives. It is not dependent merely on how much God's people *know* of His word intellectually. Knowledge apart from obedience quickly turns into religious pride. Theological arguments and differences of opinion can become the focal point of sermons and church meetings. There are times when theological differences need to be addressed. We must not open our arms so wide that we embrace error. Yet we should never forget that the Scriptures are to be obeyed, not merely dissected and debated. We ought to be as passionate about living according to the word, as we are about accurately interpreting the word. It is not possible to apply that which we have not studied, but we should never forget that once we finish our study our work has just begun. If we are to restore the anchor of God's word, we must begin with a renewed effort to apply it to our everyday lives. How we handle ourselves in the workplace and the living room must be guided by the word of God. The truths we learn from God in the Bible should not remain as only thoughts in our heads, but they should become the convictions of our hearts and the actions of our steps. Our morning reading of the Bible should become the focus of our day for the remainder of the day. To know God's words yet fail to apply them is to see the anchor but refuse to attach it to our lives. It does not ultimately matter how much knowledge we gain about the individual doctrines of the Scripture if we do not put those doctrines into practice. One can graduate first in his class at seminary and know nothing of the power of God in a life committed to obedience. May our study of God's word be renewed each day, along with a prayer to God to help us apply His word to our lives.

∞

Recognize Differences in Non-Essentials

The focus of Part Three of this book is on the need to restore the anchor of God's word. I believe the need for this to occur is as great today as it has ever been. We are experiencing the moral, economic, political, and societal deterioration that has always followed when a people reject God and set aside His word in favor of following men and their ideas. I believe the hour is late and the opportunities to reverse our course as a nation are growing fewer by the day. I am not alone in this concern. There are many others who share it with me, and I am thankful for these men and women who strive every day to conform their lives to God and His word. I am grateful for every parent who makes the sacrifices necessary to ensure they provide their children a Biblical worldview before they leave their home and begin a new home of their own. I thank God for every pastor who carefully studies and does the difficult and solitary work necessary to provide for his people the whole counsel of God. *(Acts 20.27)* I am thankful for the young people I have met who realize the dangerous direction most of their peers are heading in, and, like Daniel and his friends, resist the pull of the world to sever their tie to the anchor of the word of God. God has always had a remnant, and our day will be no exception. God will not leave Himself without a witness in the world. There will be faith on the earth when Jesus returns to gather His church to Himself. The bride will be faithfully waiting when her Groom appears.

I would like to share a few words now with the people that make up this faithful remnant. I have known many of you, but the great majority of you I will never know on this side of eternity. I have not shared your burdens, heartaches, joys, and victories. I was not there when you came to know our Lord and King. To my fellow pastors and preachers, I do not know the story of your call and all that you left to follow God's claim on your life. Despite this lack of personal knowledge, I love you all the same. My heart is full of both joy and burden when I think of you. Like Israel of old, we find ourselves in a land of spiritual exile. Our faith is being challenged and tested daily. My prayer for you and for me is that we take heart in God and take encouragement from one another. Amid these challenging days, our enemy works to separate and divide. He knows what happens to the isolated prey hunted by the ravenous lion. Satan knows that if he can divide those who stand against him, they will be much easier to conquer. Satan has been far too successful at dividing Christians for far too long, and a favorite tactic he uses is to convince Christians in one place to insist that all other Christians in all other places look exactly as they do. An insistence on uniformity on a translation. The use of wine or grape juice. Preachers that use notes or those who do not. Baptisteries or rivers. These and a host of other non-essential issues lead to division. The division over these non-essential areas of our faith serve only to weaken God's people; they do not build them up. They serve only to divide, not unite. I beg you not to spend your ministry fighting skirmishes along the borders with other Christians rather than on the front-line battle against our shared adversary.

I am not in any way suggesting that we lay down our Bibles and join hands in error. I hope what I have written in this book will bear testimony to this. It will be of no use for us to unite behind error. I have often heard it said that the most important thing is unity among churches. This statement on its own is not true. If there were a thousand churches but only one proclaiming the truth, then surely, we would not recommend that the remaining church abandon the truth so they can be in unity with the others. Would we have suggested to the Galatian church that they should not make an issue of sexual immorality so they would be in unity with a straying Corinthian church? The most important thing is the truth, not unity. Jesus' own teaching often ended with a division between those who believed and those who did not. Yet, we must be people of wisdom and discernment to know whether a division exists due to disagreement over an essential doctrine of Scripture, or if the division arises out of preferences, traditions, or other non-essentials. Uniting in error and dividing over non-essential doctrines both end up in the same place, a weakened church. Fully examining this topic would take many more chapters. My encouragement here is to search the Scriptures to discover the issues upon which they are silent. In the areas where the Bible does not speak, we should realize that there will be differences of tradition and practice that should not disrupt Christian fellowship and unity. Where God has not made a specific prescription, neither should we. He was specific with what He said, and He was specific with what He did not say. We should listen when God speaks, and we should listen when He does not. He communicates with His silence, as well as with His speech.

Chapter 15 - The Necessity of Biblical Education

"Only give heed to yourself and keep your soul diligently, so that you do not forget the things which your eyes have seen and they do not depart from your heart all the days of your life; but make them known to your sons and your grandsons. "Remember the day you stood before the LORD your God at Horeb, when the LORD said to me, 'Assemble the people to Me, that I may let them hear My words so they may learn to fear Me all the days they live on the earth, and that they may teach their children." Deuteronomy 4:9–10*

Restoring Biblical Education

Restoring a biblical education for our children is an essential element in any attempt to restore the anchor of God's Word. There is little hope of sustained success in the effort to restore the anchor of God's word if we do not address what is, I believe, the greatest threat to Christianity in America today. Some consider persecution to be the greatest threat to Christianity in America, but persecution has never represented an existential threat to faith in Christ as does a lack of Biblical education. Persecution prospers the cause of God. Rarely, if ever, does persecution lead to the extinction of faith.

Persecution arose in the early church with the killing of James. The enemies of the Gospel desired that James' execution would discourage Christians from following Christ, but it proved to have the opposite effect. Though persecution scattered the Christians, the scattering was not a detriment to the spread of the Gospel. Those who fled Jerusalem *"...went about preaching the word." (Acts 8.4).* Satan hoped to stamp out the flames of Christianity in the early church through persecution, but each attempt only fanned the flames of faith in Christ. That which began as a small spark in Jerusalem turned into a wildfire which spread across the known world. Satan's work must surely be frustrating. He desires to hurt, damage, and destroy Christians because of his searing hatred for God and those who follow him. Yet the more brutal his attempts become, the less success he enjoys.

Satan knows that comfort and acceptance is often the better tool to cause a Christian to lay aside his faith. Speaking of the liberty and acceptance that many found in America, J.M. Pendleton once said,

"Whipping and fining and imprisonment are not the only methods by which you can be injured. There is the embrace of apparent love which is the embrace of death. Error loves to ally itself with truth and the interests of truth suffer by every such alliance.[17]"

Satan could not strip Job of his faith even through all the mental, emotional, and physical pain he caused him, but he has separated countless others from their faith by making them comfortable in the world. It is not so much the pain of persecution that removes our faith, but rather it is the morphine drip of the world's pleasures and comforts that does so.

Comfort, ease, and prosperity have been the weapons of choice for Satan in our nation and, if I may be so bold, Christians have all but abandoned the effort to educate their children in the light of God's word because doing so creates massive discomfort. It is far more comfortable to hand our children over to government schools where, as a matter of policy, God's very existence is denied, than it is to assume the Biblical responsibility every Christian has to plan and watch over their children's education.

---

[17] Pendleton, J.M. (1900) An Old Landmark Reset (p.283) Nashville

King Nebuchadnezzar of Babylon knew that the key to truly subjugating an enemy nation was to take over the education of its young people. It is one thing for a nation to destroy the military power of an enemy nation. It is quite another to destroy that nation's very identity in the hearts and minds of their young people. When a nation's identity is erased and forgotten, no one remains to rebel. Destroying Israel's identity was the plan when Nebuchadnezzar took over the education of the exiled youth of Israel. The first five verses of Daniel chapter one should alarm God's people of any age and location. The military conquest was over. Israel's military could not stand against Babylon, and many Jews were exiled from Jerusalem and taken into captivity in Babylon. It was there that a much greater and far more consequential battle to destroy Israel's identity began.

"In the third year of the reign of Jehoiakim king of Judah, Nebuchadnezzar king of Babylon came to Jerusalem and besieged it. The Lord gave Jehoiakim king of Judah into his hand, along with some of the vessels of the house of God; and he brought them to the land of Shinar, to the house of his god, and he brought the vessels into the treasury of his god. Then the king ordered Ashpenaz, the chief of his officials, to bring in some of the sons of Israel, including some of the royal family and of the nobles, youths in whom was no defect, who were good-looking, showing intelligence in every branch of wisdom, endowed with understanding and discerning knowledge, and who had ability for serving in the king's court; and he ordered him to teach them the literature and language of the Chaldeans. The king appointed for them a daily ration from the king's choice food and from the wine

which he drank, and appointed that they should be educated three years, at the end of which they were to enter the king's personal service." (Dan. 1.1–5)

Nebuchadnezzar took over the education of many of the Jewish young people. In truth, He took over their entire lives. We should realize that those who control the education of a child's mind in many ways control the entire child. The king ordered that these young people read Babylonian books, speak the Babylonian language, and eat Babylonian food. They were to undergo this education for three years and then enter the king's personal service. Nebuchadnezzar was making Babylonians out of Israelites. He knew that his work to maintain control over the Jewish nation would be far easier if he turned these young Israelites into Babylonians. At the end of their three-year course of study, these Jewish youths would be nearly unidentifiable next to an ordinary Babylonian youth. They would think like a Babylonian having read Babylonian literature. They would sound like Babylonians having learned their language. They would look like Babylonians having eaten their food. For all intents and purposes, they would be Babylonian. The Jewish culture, religion, and ancestry was largely forgotten in the span of a single generation. What a dark day this must have been for the parents of these Jewish youths. What anguish of heart must have been felt when their children were taken from their homes and sent to Babylonian schools. What fear must have taken root within mothers and fathers knowing that their enemy was working to turn their children into enemies of their own people.

I write this with a broken heart and tears in my eyes. This is precisely what our enemy has orchestrated in America. Our own experience is perhaps even worse because the handing over of our children has not been at the point of a sword, but upon a soft pillow and a warm bed. We have turned our children over to an unbelieving world at the mere threat of our lost comfort, financial security, or acceptance in the world. The greatest accusation against Christianity in America might very well be the abrogation of Biblically educating our youth. Our children read only the books of the world in their education since the Bible was long ago removed. Prescribing only the books of men in their curriculum, we condemned our young people to thinking about the thoughts of other men with no awareness of the thoughts of God. We taught them to speak the language of the world. Political correctness, once the subject of mockery for parents, is now the accepted language most children speak. Even the diets of our children are largely controlled by those outside the home, just as the diets of the Israelite young people was controlled by the king.

The implications go far deeper even than just the specific materials learned. The education of our young people controls the way they think. How they think controls how they feel and how they act. The Bible plainly assures us that God is sovereign over this world, and that He will one day judge and destroy it. Yet many young people (even Christian young people) believe that man will be responsible for the end of the earth. I wonder if any who are trumpeting their views of the end of the earth because of man's behavior have ever stopped to consider the pressure they are placing on the Millennial generation. The average Millennial today believes that if they do not fix what previous generations have broken, then the world will literally melt away beneath their feet. It is the height of arrogance, blindness, and irrationality. Yet it is what we have allowed the world to teach our children, and it is sadly what most of them appear to believe.

Many might console themselves with the thought that their children are an exception to the rule. They believe that *their* children will somehow be stronger, smarter, loved more, or that God will ensure that they are not swayed by the foolishness of the world because they are *our* children. To this I offer the reminder that God commanded His people to educate their children in His light and in His word. If we fail in our obedience to this command, we will not have God to blame for our failure, and we must not expect God to deliver us from our own willful disobedience. To ask God to get us out of the consequences of our sin is tantamount to asking God to act contrary to His own nature. He has told us that what we reap is nothing more or less than what we have sown. *(Gal. 6.7)*

A dangerous pride has taken root in our hearts when we think our children will stand in the face of a worldly education. It is abundantly clear that the majority have not. I believe that most Christian parents would be shocked to hear what their children honestly believe regarding the cultural issues of our day. Sticking our heads in the sand, we continue to be willing accessories to the removal of the Christian identity among our own youth.

The astute Bible student would point out that even amid

Nebuchadnezzar's goals, Daniel, Hananiah, Mishael, and Azariah remained faithful to God. The faithfulness of these four young men might be considered a defense for sending our children to schools that know not God. Two points should be kept in view before making this leap in logic.First, if the Israelites were given a choice in the matter, it is highly unlikely that they would have willingly sent their children to Babylonian schools to learn how to be Babylonians when God had specifically commanded them to teach their children what it meant to be among the nation that Jehovah called His own. The Jewish people knew that God had dealt with their nation in a special and unique way. They knew that it was through their national identity that the world would see the true and living God of Heaven and Earth. One can lay many charges against Israel in the Old Testament, but one charge that cannot be made is a misunderstanding that they were God's nation on earth and called to be different and separate from all the other nations of the world. For us to have a choice, and willingly give our children a worldly education rather than one guided by God and His word, betrays where our own hearts really are.

Secondly, Daniel and his three companions were clearly exceptions to the rule. Of all the Hebrew children Nebuchadnezzar took, we know of only these four who remained faithful. We find further support of their status as exceptions when Israel was given the opportunity to return to Jerusalem. Of the millions of Jews in Babylon, only a small fraction chose to return home to Israel, and the rest remained in Babylon. Having built comfortable lives and having become more Babylonian than Jewish, they saw no need to make the difficult journey home to Jerusalem. That the city and its walls laid in ruins was of no concern to them. Business was good in Babylon and their children were prospering there. Why upset such a comfortable life for a life filled with danger, sacrifice, and hard work? Who would wish that upon their children? We note however, that *exceptions* to the rule do not invalidate the *rule*. Because four young men proved faithful does not mean that most did not. Because a few here and there, through God's grace and mercy, remain faithful in the face of the worldly education they receive does not mean that the vast majority are not fleeing the church in droves.

I am praying for many Daniel's, Hananiah's, Mishael's, and Azariah's in our day. Young people who desire with all their hearts to be like Christ and not the world. Young men and women who desire to speak the language of love and godliness and not the language of hate and wickedness spoken by the world. I am praying for young parents who refuse to have their children's minds filled with the lies of the enemy when they are so fragile and impressionable. I believe God will answer this prayer. Yet even an answered prayer from God that there will be exceptions does not eliminate the immense damage caused by the rule. We have robbed the children of this nation from a true education. An education that provides answers in God rather than empty questions from man. We lose an incredible opportunity to point children to God when we tell them that numbers are infinite but tell them nothing of the infinite God who contains them all. How blind is every history lesson that does not point out the hand of Providence that has watched over the world since it began? What irrational silliness would we save our children from if we set before them God's creation of the world as simple truth? If we did, perhaps they would not believe the sheer lunacy that something can come from nothing. How much happier might they be knowing that God created them on purpose, and for a purpose, and that they are not the result of chaotic and random chance? How much more like young men and women might they behave if they were told that they are not animals, but human beings created in the image of God Himself? How much more slowly might a young lady bring an end to the life of her unborn child if she knew that the life within her was a creation of God, and not a mere choice she makes. On and on these questions could go. My heart breaks for how we have failed the generation behind us. We have given them an education far below the station God would have men and women occupy.

I realize my tone might sound harsh. You might feel as though I am being unfair. Harshness and unfairness are not my aim, but I do desire to offer a passionate plea for those who believe in God's word to awaken to the battle that has been waging while the vast majority of us have been lulled to sleep in the comfortable bed called Christianity in America. Church for most Christians in America is defined by the weekly services conducted in the church building, and this view has taken us to a place where any attempt to meddle in our lives outside of those services is unwelcome. Most are quickly offended and begin justifying their actions by saying that what they do outside of church is not anyone's business but their own. This view might be the accepted norm today, but it is foreign to Scripture.

The Lost Anchor

We have largely lost the battle for our young people under the cover that their education is separate from their Christianity. When Christianity loses control of the schoolhouse, it is only a matter of time before the church house will be empty and a mere shell of its former self. The deepest cuts in the rope that once tied us to the anchor of God's word have not been made by swords of persecution, but by crayons and pencils in classrooms across the country. Until we take control once again of our children's education, I fear that any hope to restore the Bible to its rightful place in our nation will be ineffective. We simply cannot expect to combat the thirty plus hours of worldly education, and the many hours spent steeped in this world's culture, with a thirty-minute Sunday School lesson and perhaps a forty-five-minute sermon on Sundays. To believe this is to cling to a desperate hope that has no basis in reason, or precedence in Scripture.

Chapter 16 - The Need for Perseverance

"Blessed is a man who perseveres under trial; for once he has been approved, he will receive the crown of life which the Lord has promised to those who love Him." James 1:12

We examined the evidence of our nation's disconnection from the anchor of truth in the opening chapters of this book. That evidence is overwhelming. So much so that individual Christians and even entire churches can become discouraged. With each passing day, there seems to be some new headline that reveals the drift of our nation away from God. As children of God, we must always guard our hearts against discouragement and despair Individual Christians and churches have lost many battles without a fight because they thought the situation so hopeless that they did not give God a chance to show Himself to be the loving, omniscient, and omnipotent God that He is. Discouragement is only one small step away from surrender, and the Christian must never surrender. We must never stop striving to steer the ship back to the anchor of God's word. We must never forget that when things seem the most hopeless in our eyes is often the very moment that God delivers. We must never assume that God will not, or cannot, right what is wrong. We must trust that success will eventually find those who seek God with a diligent and sincere heart.

We have ample evidence in history, and likely our own lives for this outlook. It was not until the people of Israel were between Pharaoh's army on one side and an impassable Red Sea on the other that God delivered. It was not until Gideon's army was small enough that the victory could be attributed to God alone that the battle was won. *(Jg. 2.2-7)* God whittled Gideon's army down from 32,000 to 300 and then sent them into the fight. Those holding to the Bible's place as the source of absolute truth in the world may be a minority today, but with God, the problem is often that there are too many rather than too few. When men congregate in great numbers, they often place their trust in their numbers and not in God. When we can go about our days without feeling a deep sense of our complete need for God, something is missing. When a church can go through every step of their service without the Spirit intervening, something is missing. The Christian life is a paradox of complete and total helplessness in ourselves, combined with a complete and total assurance and confidence in God.

It was not until I saw the hopelessness of my case without

Christ that I repented and placed my trust completely in Christ and was saved. Our unwillingness to cling to God until we have no other option remaining to us is a testimony of our belligerent insistence to trust in ourselves. When God removes from us all other options, He demonstrates His graciousness and it is a testimony to His inestimable benevolence. When good health causes us to forget God, sickness is not a curse, but a blessing. When financial stability gives us peace of mind rather than God, it is the goodness of God that allows our wealth to be taken away. When we anchor our lives to anything that is passing, transient, or uncertain, God is not punishing us when He takes those things from us. It is not God's anger that takes from us the worldly ease and comfort we desire. It is His love that does so.

I mention these things to point out that the desperate condition our nation is presently in, is no reason to give up hope in God. It is true, if things continue as they are, that it could mean the end of this great experiment called the United States, but it might also mean that God is allowing us to get to the end of our rope so we will have nothing left to hold on to but Him. Can you imagine the glory it would bring our great God if we turned once again back to Him as a nation? Can you hear the shouts of praise to our God if we once again heard our children come home and tell us what they learned about God when they studied their science, history and math? Can you imagine the peace that would settle over our nation once again if our politicians openly admitted that they, like all men, are in the hands of God? What great advances might we once again see in our nation if we were to pursue afresh the subduing of the earth in obedience to God's command, instead of a desire for mere personal gain? There will always be a struggle on this side of eternity, but what blessings might God shower upon us if we turned back to Him? What might we see if we took God at His word when He tells us, "*...test me now in this, if I will not open for you the windows of heaven and pour out for you a blessing until it overflows." (Mal. 3.10)*

There are two paths ahead of us. The first path is for our nation to reconnect to the anchor of God's word. On such a path, the blessings we would enjoy stretch language to its breaking point. The second path is that our nation continues to drift until it vanishes over the horizon of history and is quickly forgotten. We know that God's church will never vanish over that horizon. She will remain afloat through all the storms on the sea of time through which she sails. The church has enjoyed largely calm seas in the United States, but the waves are growing larger and the skies are growing darker. Persecution is rising, and the threat of its continued increase is real. But either of these two paths will find God's people attached firmly to God's word.

I pray earnestly that God would spare our nation and re-establish us upon the anchor of His word. Yet our attachment as individuals and as churches is not dependent on what our nation does. The clear evidence of God's hand in the establishment of our nation should not cause us to think He will never allow it to fall. He gives nations a choice just as He gives individuals a choice. That choice is to follow Him or to follow something else. We must take care that we do not equate our nation with the church. This nation has been a haven for the church for many years, but it has never been the church. The freedom's and Christian principles of this nation have been worth fighting and dying for. Many have done so, and these men and women should be honored and remembered with deep and inexpressible gratitude. However, if this nation turns completely from God, then our allegiance must remain with God and His people, not this nation.

Do not misread these thoughts. I sincerely hope that God will spare our great country -- this land of the free and the home of the brave. I pray for Him to move us back towards Himself and away from ourselves. I love our country. The United States has provided more hope and peace to more people than any other nation in history. As distant as we now are from God, we remain a light to the world. However, it appears as well that our light is growing dimmer, and it is threatening to go out completely. Because of this, my love for God must exceed my love for my country, and so too must yours. The turning back to God that we desire will not happen without men and women who will challenge the direction in which we are heading, and the new identity absent of God of which we are taking.

The present spiritual darkness that blankets our land did not appear overnight. It has taken many decades for us to find ourselves this far from where we started. Little by little, the enemy sowed and sold one lie after another, which diverted us from the path of life and sent us down the path of destruction. It is impossible to say for certain how much of the path lies ahead of us before we reach the cliff, but surely it must be in view. Yet, we are so enamored by the temporary pleasures of this path of destruction, we continue to walk it. Spoiled with worldly treasures and comforts like no other people in history, we refuse to do the difficult and sacrificial work necessary to turn around and begin again to walk in the path of life. Each step takes us closer to our own destruction, and yet we keep walking. We continue to elect politicians who do not fear God. We continue to send our children to the world for their education and expect them to avoid becoming a world-ling. We avoid the reading of our Bibles. We neglect daily prayer and fellowship with God and His people. We believe we are making advances in our lives while our spiritual condition deteriorates more and more each day. We judge ourselves by ourselves and then confess ourselves wise when we have become fools. *(2 Cor. 10.12, Rom. 1.22)*

I do not say these things to offend. I say them to raise an alarm. The alarms that wake us up in the morning are not typically welcome. We groggily turn them off and pull ourselves out of our soft, warm beds when all we want to do is go back to sleep. Or we hit the snooze button, attempting to squeeze in just a little more rest before the day begins. We sometimes hit the snooze button again and again, and we allow our weariness to rule rather than our determination to rise from bed and redeem the day. It is time for those of us who hear the alarm to rise from sleep. To shake the grogginess and lethargy of worldliness from our hearts, minds, and bodies. To stop debating with ourselves whether we will get up, and just get up. To prepare ourselves for the day ahead. To turn to our families, friends, and neighbors, and cry out to them to rise from their own slumbering. The moments of our lives are passing quickly. The time is short. The work is great, and it will not get done while we remain asleep in our beds.

The distance we have traveled in the wrong direction should prepare us for the time and effort it will take to get back to where we started. Anything is possible with God. He could restore us in an instant should He desire to do so, but the witness of Scripture and history points us to the likelihood that we will have to retake the ground we have lost one step at a time. Retaking that ground will likely take many years and decades. We are not engaged in a battle that will be over within a matter of a few days, weeks, or even years. It is a battle that we will be engaged in for the rest of our lives. I am confident that we can retake the ground, but it is improbable that we will regain it all in my lifetime. I am prayerful and hopeful that my children's generation and their children after them will retake lost ground when my time in the fight is over. If you are among those future generations I am now writing of, and God has placed this book in your hands many years from now and my body lies cold in the grave, I pray these words will drive you toward God and a godly life. Toward the anchor of God's word. What a treasure in Heaven such a thing would be. A treasure I will place at the feet of my Savior, my King, and my God and thank him with tears of joy forever and ever that I was able to be even a weak vessel in His almighty hands.

The Lost Anchor

The effort to restore the anchor of God's word will require great effort because of the distance we have gone in the wrong direction, and patience will be necessary because the effort will require the doing of many *little things consistently*, more than the doing a *few great things occasionally*. We all want to be the hero who slays Goliath when the entire world is watching, but few of us want to be the lone shepherd on the hillside when the lion and the bear show up. Life is about doing the right small things consistently much more than doing great things inconsistently. We will not find our way back to the anchor of God's word because a minister preaches a sermon for the ages. There will be no substitute for taking one step at a time, day after day, week after week, and year after year toward God and His word. Our generation's microwave mindset is an enemy of this outlook. Seeing the distance that we must travel to return to God, many turn back having never taken even the first step. It is at times like these that we must remember that the most important step in a long journey is the next one. Do not fail to take the first step because you are fearful or uncertain of what the next step will be. God has promised to provide the strength and direction you need, but He often does so one step at a time.

It should encourage us though that we often overestimate what we can accomplish in one year and underestimate what we can accomplish in five years. Albert Einstein once said that the most powerful force in the world is compounding interest. Anyone who has been on the wrong side of the interest rate as a borrower knows this is true. This principle applies to the results of our investments with our time as well as it does with our financial investments. When we make small but relentlessly consistent investments in the reading of our Bibles and in prayer, over time that investment will build on itself. The return on that investment will be far greater than we could ever imagine, but we too often prefer that the return on our investment happen quickly, and with only a small sacrifice on our part. But life does not work this way and it never has. As we consider the effort and time it will take to regain the spiritual ground we have lost, I pray we do not grow weary in the effort. *(2 Thes. 3.13)* If we do, we will never again find ourselves tied securely to the anchor of the Bible.

Chapter 17 - The Word Became Flesh

"And the Word was made flesh, and dwelt among us, (and we beheld his glory, the glory as of the only begotten of the Father,) full of grace and truth." John 1:14

The Scriptures are the very words of God to man and the source of absolute truth in the world. We find in the Bible what we find nowhere else -- a perfect treasure and record of truth. It would be an enormous oversight, however, if we do not realize that the truth is ultimately a *Person*. The Bible itself tells us this in John 14:6 when Jesus stated that He is the truth. The Bible is not an end in itself, but it does show us the truth, bring us to the truth, and bears witness to the truth. Yet the Bible is not the truth itself. This is not to say that the Bible is not true. I have said otherwise repeatedly throughout this book, but it is to say that there is something beyond the words on the pages of Scripture. There is a *Person* of whom all the Scripture speaks, and to whom all Scripture points. That Person is Jesus Christ, the Son of God. To know the truth is to know Christ. To see the truth is to see Christ. To understand the Bible is to understand Christ. The reverse of these things is also true. If we do not know Christ, we do not know the truth. If we do not see Christ, we are blind to the truth. A failure to understand Christ, is a failure to understand truth.

We must therefore exercise caution in our pursuit of restoring the Scripture to our land. We must be careful that we do not pursue the Bible apart from pursuing Christ. Our goal is not only to restore the anchor of the Bible in our land, it is to restore the very presence of God among us in the Person of His Son through the working of the Holy Spirit. We will not accomplish this goal without the Bible, but we will fail to accomplish the ultimate goal if we restore the Bible in our lives but fail to restore Christ as well. We can restore a habit of daily Bible reading without exchanging a single word with God in prayer. If we do this, however, we will have missed the entire point of the Bible. We will not see the Person who is the ultimate and absolute truth in the universe. The Bible is a priceless gift from God and there is no amount of treasure in this world that would equal the value of the Bible. Yet, it is possible to misuse the gifts of God and the Bible is no exception.

∞

Misused Gifts of God

Man's misuse of the gifts of God appears again and again in the Bible. Much of the sin we commit originates from a misuse of a gift that God has given. The misuse of money, work, and sex, all gifts from God, constitute many of the sins we struggle with in our lives. We can even misuse the very things God has given to remind us of Him.

One of the most alarming examples of a misuse of a gift of God is found in 1st Samuel chapter four. The Israelites were once again in conflict with the Philistines. Four thousand men had died in the opening skirmish of the battle. The sons of Eli (the High Priest), Hophni and Phinehas, along with the elders of Israel, misused the Ark of the Covenant for their own purposes in a desperate and misguided attempt to get God on their side. In their religious superstition, they believed the Ark would allow them to tap into the power of God to overcome their enemy. The fundamental problem with their plan was that God was not with them in this fight, and He is not a God who can be manipulated and controlled by men, even with things He has given to them.

This battle was one that Israel had provoked. There is no evidence that they had consulted God to learn His will regarding the Philistines, or whether they should go out to fight on this day or not. Perhaps they assumed that God wanted them to overcome their enemies. After all, were they not God's people? Had God not said so throughout the Old Testament? God, however, often used foreign nations in the Old Testament to discipline His people. Sometimes, Israel was to fight, but there were also times when they were to submit to their enemies and accept God's punishment. At the battle of Aphek, there appeared to be no desire to seek God's counsel and they found themselves in a fight they could not win. Following their reckless and spiritually uninformed plan, they attempted to pull God into the fight by using a gift He had given them in the Ark of the Covenant.

Israel reveals their misguided thoughts about the Ark when they say,

"Why has the LORD defeated us today before the Philistines? Let us take to ourselves from Shiloh the ark of the covenant of the LORD, that it may come among us and deliver us from the power of our enemies." (1 Sam. 4.3)

Notice carefully the words that betray their error. Israel thought to take the Ark of the Lord to *themselves*. They believed that they could control God by controlling the object He had given them as the gift that symbolized and affirmed His presence among them. They also thought the ark of the Lord itself would save them. Their trust was not that God would save them. Instead, they placed their trust in a gift God had given them. As precious a gift as the Ark was, without the approval and actual presence of God, it was nothing more than an ornate religious artifact. The results of this strategy were catastrophic for Israel. 1 Samuel 4.10-11 records

The Lost Anchor

the sad results of their defeat.

"10 So the Philistines fought and Israel was defeated, and every man fled to his tent; and the slaughter was very great, for there fell of Israel thirty thousand foot soldiers. 11 And the ark of God was taken; and the two sons of Eli, Hophni and Phinehas, died." (1 Sam. 4.10-11)

When Eli heard that his sons had died and the Philistines had taken the Ark, he fell from his seat and died. (*1 Sam. 4.12-18*). Eli's daughter-in-law gave birth to a son at the close of the battle and named him Ichabod, referring to the departure of God's glory from Israel. (*1 Sam. 4.19-22*) The attempt to misuse a gift of God ended in great tragedy for Eli, Hophni, Phinehas, and all of Israel. The same thing happens today when we attempt to misuse the gifts God has given us. For this reason, we must not misuse the Bible.

Abraham provides a positive example of how to view and hold the gifts that God gives. In one of the most well-known stories in the Old Testament, God commands Abraham to sacrifice Isaac. Isaac was the gift that God had promised to Abraham. He was a miracle child, born far past the time that Abraham and Sarah should have been able to have children. There was no doubt in Abraham's mind that God had come through on His promise when Isaac was born. God, however, is always interested in determining if we treasure Him more than we treasure His gifts, and this was the test for Abraham; a test which he passed with flying colors. It was not until Abraham had Isaac bound on the altar with the knife ready to strike that God stopped him. God said to Abraham,

"Do not stretch out your hand against the lad, and do nothing to him; for now I know that you fear God, since you have not withheld your son, your only son, from Me." (Gen. 22.12)

Abraham loved his son Isaac deeply. We can only imagine the turmoil and spiritual warfare that must have been raging in his mind and heart, but in the end, Abraham chose God above God's gift.

Some struggle with this story. They see moral implications that challenge the Bible's assertion that God is good. God's actions are deemed unfair here, but we should remember that God stayed Abraham's hand before he took Isaac's life. God provided an alternative sacrifice in place of Isaac.

"Then Abraham raised his eyes and looked, and behold, behind him a ram caught in the thicket by his horns; and Abraham went and took the ram and offered him up for a burnt offering in the place of his son." (Gen. 22.13)

Some wonder why a person would be so dedicated to God that they would be willing to give up their own children. What would drive a person to forsake all and follow Christ? We see the answer when we realize that God did not stay His own hand when He sent His Son to the cross. There was no other sacrifice provided in the place of His Son. Even though Jesus called to Him multiple times to remove the cup of His suffering, God did not spare His own Son. Instead, He gave Him to you, to me, and to everyone. He gave His Son up to the cross, so that He might bring us up to Himself. He allowed His Son to die, so that you and I might live. We give up all that we have so that we might be with God because God gave up His only Son to be with us. With the song writer we sing, *"Take the whole world, but give me Jesus."* It is God we seek, not just His gifts. It is God we must have a relationship with, not just His blessings. God wants to shower us with His *presence*, not just His *treasures*. The Bible is a sure anchor in an unsteady world, but it is only fully so if it binds us to the Person of Christ.

The Greater Purpose

It is easy to use the Bible as the Israelites used the Ark. Hollywood portrays the priest holding a Bible out in front of him as he fends off the demons bent on destruction. Pastors hide their lack of a personal knowledge of God behind their academic knowledge of the Bible. We think the leather, ink, and paper in our Bible's hold a mystical power that does not exist. People are told that merely repeating certain words found in the Bible have the power to save, to heal, or to grant riches. But this is a belief in mysticism and superstition, not God. The Bible bears witness to the Person who is omniscient, omnipotent, and omnipresent, but it is not itself omniscient, omnipotent, and omnipresent. The Bible's testimony of the One who is all these things is completely true, but it is a witness to, and about, another, and not itself.

I fear there are many who may have a personal relationship

with the Bible but have no relationship at all with the God of the Bible. To these I ask, *"What does the Bible itself say we will do in Heaven for eternity?"* Heaven will not be an unending Bible study. It will be an unending experience of the presence of God. This God that we came to know personally in this life. This God who became more to us than all the other things in our lives, including the very gifts He gave. We need to restore the anchor of God's word in our land, but the reason we need to do so is for the greater purpose of restoring God's presence in our lives. If we simply restore the Bible and not the Person of Christ, we might improve our morality by leaps and bounds, but we will not improve our hearts at all. And it is our hearts that God is after, not merely our behavior. *(Ps. 119.34, Pro. 23.26)* Does God have your heart? Or does He merely have your behavior? The difference is not small. It is a difference measured by eternity. When you read the Bible, are you satisfied with knowing the words only? Or does your soul long for the One about whom those words speak? The absolute truth is the Person of Christ. The Bible reveals Him, but it can never replace Him.

Closing Thoughts

My prayer is that God has used this work to encourage you to make the Bible the anchor of your life, to restore it if you have let it go, or perhaps re-establish your grip if it has loosened over time. If just one person takes from this book a longing to dig deeper into the word of God than they ever have before, then I will consider the time and effort spent in its preparation a small price for such a glorious result. If you now want to do little more than open your Bible, begin to read, and glorify God, then I rejoice with you in the great journey that is ahead of you.

If there are mistakes in this book, and surely there are, attribute those to the author alone. I had much assistance with this book, but the responsibility is ultimately mine, and not on those who provided me with much-needed help. My subject from the beginning to the end has been far above me. The word of God is like a mountain that can be admired and even partly ascended but can never be fully conquered. We will never reach the summit until we leave this world. Until then, may we all strain with holy and humble might to climb as high as we can.

Finally, thank you for taking your time to read this book. You will have discovered by now that I am not a gifted writer, but God can do great things with small things. What a comfort that knowledge is for those of us who are small. Yet we need good books today, and though I knew from the beginning I could not provide a *good book* for the world and for God's people, I knew I could at least give them a book *about* the *greatest book.* If this book inspires those of you who do have the gift of writing to put pen to paper to tell of the excellencies of God, then I would bask in great delight in your shadow. To any who might be called by God to write...read continually, read broadly, pray diligently, study hard, prepare yourself for the work...and then write what God has placed within you.

May God bless you, and all His people everywhere.

Kent Welch

Made in the USA
Columbia, SC
08 February 2021